Excellence
in
First-Year Writing
2016/2017

The English Department Writing Program
and
The Gayle Morris Sweetland Center for Writing

Edited by
Dana Nichols

Published in 2017 by Michigan Publishing
University of Michigan Library

Permission is required to reproduce material from this title in other
publications, coursepacks, electronic products, and other media.

Please send permission requests to:

Michigan Publishing
1210 Buhr Building
839 Greene Street
Ann Arbor, MI 48104
lib.pod@umich.edu

ISBN 978-1-60785-416-6

Table of Contents

Excellence in First-Year Writing

Excellence in First-Year Writing 2016/2017

EDWP Writing Prize Chairs

Anne Charlotte Mecklenburg

Molly Parsons

EDWP Writing Prize Committee

John F. Buckley

Catherine Cassel

Rachel Cawkwell

Maia Farrar

Kyle Frisina

Mika Kennedy

Naitnaphit Limlamai

Sarah Linwick

Emily McLaughlin

Adrienne Raw

Amanda Rybin Koob

Michelle Sprouse

Bonnie Tucker

Sweetland Writing Prize Chair

Dana Nichols

Sweetland Writing Prize Committee

Paul Barron

Scott Beal

Gina Brandolino

Louis Cicciarelli

T Hetzel

Lillian Li

Shelley Manis

Raymond McDaniel

Christine Modey

Dana Nichols

Simone Sessolo

Naomi Silver

Carol Tell

Administrative Support

Laura Schulyer

Aaron Valdez

Winners List

Feinberg Family Prize for Excellence in First-Year Writing

Julia Dreher, "The Conscious and Unconscious Natures of Belief"
Nominated by Adam Sneed, English 125

Jaylin Herskovitz, "The Complexity of Grief"
Nominated by Tiffany Ball, English 125

Jason Jin, "Music for Non-musicians"
Nominated by Aaron Burch, English 125

Matt Kelley/Granader Family Prize for Excellence in First-Year Writing

Serena Scholz, "The Helsinki Waste Closet Incident"
Nominated by Louis Cicciarelli, LHSP 125

Bailey Stein, "Coins"
Nominated by Carol Tell, LHSP 125

Granader Family Prize for Excellence in Multilingual Writing

Xiaowei Ou, "The Molecular Connection between Chemistry and Learning Astronomy"
Nominated by Shuwen Li, Writing 120

Fengyi Tong, "Comparative Analysis of Two Print Advertisements"
Nominated by Scott Beal, Writing 120

Granader Family Prize for Outstanding Writing Portfolio

Stephanie Bloom
Nominated by Gina Brandolino, Writing 100

Miles Honey
Nominated by Julie Babcock, Writing 100

Feinberg Family Prize nominees

Student Name	Instructor Name
Tosin Adeyemi	Molly Dickinson
Tara Andrews	Margo Kolenda
James Bargmann	Megan Behrend
Jenna Barlage	Elizabeth McAdams
Roxanne Blanchette	Joey Gamble
Brielle Bonetti	Katie Willingham
Matthew Boyle	Michelle Sprouse
Shea Carponter-Broderick	Michelle Sprouse
Anna Clark	Marlin Jenkins
Jessica Cummings	Kristen Roupenian
Julia Dreher	Adam Sneed
Shannon Elkins	Xiaoxi Zhang
Sarah Fan	Megan Behrend
Alex Fial	Aaron Burch
Daniel Fuhrer	Cecilia Morales
Bianca Gallina	Alicia Stevers
Marguerite Harris	Kristen Roupenian
Jaylin Herskovitz	Tiffany Ball
Alex Hunt	Adrienne Raw
Audrey Hunt	Joey Gamble
Sarah Hussain	Lucy Hartley
Courtney Jacobsen	Yasin Abdul-Muqit
Jamie Jacobson	Naitnaphit Limlamai
Jason Jin	Aaron Burch
Elizabeth John	Cecilia Morales
Andrew Kassa	Emily McLaughlin
Zoe Kolender	Joey Gamble
Rhea Kulkarni	John F. Buckley
Rob Lawrence	Kristin vanEyk

Feinberg Family Prize nominees

Student Name	Instructor Name
Cameron Leitz	Alicia Stevers
Sarah Lime	Megan Behrend
Josephine Luttman	Charles Taylor
Eli Masjedi	Sarah Mass
CJ Mayer	Chris McCormick
Ryan Miller	Megan Behrend
Abbie Moccio	Marlin Jenkins
Lily Morris	Chris McCormick
Ryan Myers	John F. Buckley
Hannah Nelson	Kyle C. Frisina
Elsy Nouna	Emily McLaughlin
Nick Panagakis	John F. Buckley
Jonathan Pham	David Martin
Harlan Rappaport	Aaron Burch
Samantha Searles	Cecilia Morales
Jakob Sheridan	K. E. Allen
Tiffany Sheu	Yasin Abdul-Muqit
Alexis Smith	Aaron Burch
Laurel Sparks	K. E. Allen
Elizabeth Stolze	John F. Buckley
Emily Stringham	Marlin Jenkins
Katherine Stroud	Yasin Abdul-Muqit
Gina Vasey	Tiffany Ball
Jacob Voyzey	Sarah Mass
Hannah Wang	Xiaoxi Zhang
Jacob Wexler	Emily McLaughlin
Tiffany Wheeler	John F. Buckley
Erika Yasuda	John F. Buckley

Matt Kelley/Granader Family Prize nominees

Student Name	Instructor Name
Jenna Barlage	Elizabeth McAdams
Cecelia Batterbee	Van Tu
Jeremy D'silva	Van Tu
Clare Francis	Yael Kenan
Isabella Gierlinger	Carrie Wood
Sam Groh	Lindsay Helfman
Ian Harris	Vincenzo Salvatore
Natalia Jenuwine	Bree Doering
Jolie Moray	Scott Beal
Lily Morris	Chris McCormick
Meghann Norden-Bright	Lauren Benjamin
Mary Oseguera	Paul Barron
Sage Renstrom-Richards	Alex Elkins
Caralyn Ryan	Louis Cicciarelli
Sarah Saks-Fithian	Paul Barron
Serena Scholz	Will Stroebel
Emily Shiau	Carol Tell
Verity Sturm	Carrie Wood
Sakina Tinwala	Scott Beal
Grace Wilkins	Lauren Benjamin
Connor Young	Rachel Cawkwell
Qhoe Yun	Will Stroebel
Anne Zhao	Vincenzo Salvatore

Granader Family Portfolio Prize nominees

Student Name	Instructor Name
Vedant Agrawal	Larissa Sano
Yuwei Bao	Scott Beal
Stephanie Bloom	Gina Brandolino
Alan Chu	Lillian Li
Lorna Courtney	Stephanie Moody
Giovanna Fortuna	Julie Babcock
Claire Freimark	Catherine Cassel
Miles Honey	Julie Babcock
Killian Kerr	Lillian Li
Zenani Kettle	Ali Shapiro
Yun-Yu Liu	Stephanie Moody
Yuning Liu	Simone Sessolo
Chiara Lommer	Simone Sessolo
Sarah Lipshultz	Suzanne Drapeau
Yolanda Marti	Gina Brandolino
Alia Meliki	T Hetzel
James Ryan Morrison	T Hetzel
Emma Spencer	Catherine Cassel
Jiayu (Sherry) Zhang	Scott Beal

Granader Family Multilingual Prize nominees

Student Name	Instructor Name
Yaqi Hu	Colin Corrigan
Nayeon (Grace) Kwon	Scott Beal
Xiaoyu Li	Shuwen Li
Moeka Matsuo	Scott Beal
Xiaowei Ou	Shuwen Li
Fengyi Tong	Scott Beal
Ziyi Wu	Shuwen Li

Introduction

When they enter the University, students share the common experience of taking a required first-year writing course. With the help of their instructors, they learn to develop evidence-based arguments, a skill they can take with them to many other courses. They also learn strategies for crafting effective introductions, elaborating on ideas, and teasing out implications. Perhaps most important, participating in peer review sessions and conferences with instructors helps students to recognize the social dimensions of writing and the crucial distinction between proofreading and actually revising.

The pages that follow offer a sampling of some of the best writing produced in first-year writing classes. Following a tradition started in 2010, instructors in the English Department Writing Program and the Sweetland Center for Writing nominate students whose writing exemplifies exceptional quality. Thanks to generous support from the Granader family along with Andrew Feinberg and Stacia Smith, each winning writer receives a cash prize, and his/her essay is published in this book and its online companion. We have much to learn from the ways in which these inspiring, prize-winning essays formulate compelling questions, engage in dialogue with other thinkers, incorporate persuasive evidence, express poetic and powerful insights, and participate in meaningful conversations.

The careful editing of Dana Nichols and the design work of Aaron Valdez show these award-winning essays to best advantage. Sweetland faculty members Naomi Silver, Paul Barron, Louis Cicciarelli, T Hetzel, Carol Tell, and Dana Nichols read for the Portfolio Prize. Faculty readers for the Kelley/Granader prize were Raymond McDaniel, Gina Brandolino, Scott Beal, Christine Modey, Lillian

Li, and Dana Nichols. Shelley Manis and Simone Sessolo read essays submitted for the Multilingual Prize.

The following members of the EDWP community generously served as readers for the Feinberg Prize: John Buckley, Catherine Cassel, Rachel Cawkwell, Maia Farrar, Kyle Frisina, Mika Kennedy, Naitnaphit Limlamai, Sarah Linwick, Emily McLaughlin, Adrienne Raw, Amanda Robyn Koob, Michelle Sprouse, Bonnie Tucker, and Crystal Yin Lie. We are very grateful to all of these readers, whose gifts of feedback and time made this collection possible.

The many instructors who encouraged, supported, and nominated their students deserve our thanks as well. Day after day, these instructors helped their students to see themselves as writers.

Finally, we celebrate all the students who submitted essays for these writing prizes. Many took risks by trying new approaches, exploring unfamiliar concepts, and sharing unpolished drafts, and in doing so, they contributed to the intellectual energy and creativity of their classes and our campus.

Anne Ruggles Gere, Director, Sweetland Center for Writing
Megan Sweeney, Director, English Department Writing Program

Feinberg Family Prize for Excellence in First-Year Writing

On behalf of the selection committee, we are pleased to introduce the three winners of the 2016 Feinberg Family Prize for Excellence in First-Year Composition. These essays were originally written in English 124 and 125 during the 2016 calendar year, and were considered by their instructors to best represent the excellent work of our students in the English Department Writing Program (EDWP).

This year we had an impressive 59 nominations in three primary categories: analytic argument, narrative argument, and research-based argument. Our judges therefore had a very difficult task this year, as they so often do. Each of the nominated essays demonstrated a thoughtfulness and willingness to take intellectual risks that made them a true pleasure to read.

The three winners impressed the judges with their nuanced approach to their subjects, their clear articulation of argumentative stakes, and their agile negotiation of different types of evidence. The winning analytic argument takes up the subject of belief-formation that balances competing demands of ethics and practicality and deftly reveals connections among a selection of sophisticated source material. From the narrative argument category, we present an essay that crisply and dynamically weaves the author's description of an orchestral piece together with an argument about why we pursue non-professional endeavors. And, finally, from the research-based argument category, the winning essay situates Alison Bechdel's *Fun Home* in the context of shifting theoretical and cultural approaches to grief, offering a compelling reading of Bechdel's piece while exploring the nature of a complex human experience. All three of this year's winners approached their respective genres with an eye toward holding together messy and sometimes contradictory ideas.

The co-chairs would like to thank everyone -- students, instructors, and judges -- who contributed to this year's Feinberg Prize. We were very thankful for this opportunity to reflect on the qualities we most admire and hope to cultivate in first-year student writing. Through the generous permission of the Prize winners, we are delighted to offer here, in this collection, a glimpse of the excellent work we see day-to- day and semester-to- semester from students and instructors in Michigan's introductory writing classes.

Anne-Charlotte Mecklenburg and Molly Parsons
Co-Chairs of the Feinberg Family Prize for Excellence in First-Year Writing Committee
Graduate Student Mentors, English Department Writing Program

The Conscious and Unconscious Natures of Belief

Julia Dreher
From English 125
Nominated by Adam Sneed

This is the first of four excellent essays Julia wrote for our English 125 class. In this assignment, students were asked to perform a critique of William K. Clifford's classic essay, "The Ethics of Belief." There Clifford puts forth an uncompromising argument for the absolute necessity of gathering sufficient evidence for any and every belief. Clifford's essay could be said to establish a normative ideal for evidence-based belief, one to which we might all hope to aspire in a perfect world of evidence-based reasoning but which is clearly in tension with the actual psychology of belief. Students were asked to select an essay which seems to pose a challenge to this normative ideal, stage an intervention between the two texts, and draw on that intervention to arrive at a modified ethics of belief.

Julia's essay stands out for many reasons. It stages a complex intervention between two very different kinds of argument and clarifies the stakes of that intervention with an impressive control and nuance. But perhaps what I admire most about the essay is how it successfully completes the "arc" of its critical intervention. Julia does not stop her inquiry once she exposes the limitations of Clifford's ethical argument, a common trap laid by critique as a form. Rather, she continues past this negative moment and works to construct a qualified account of Clifford's ethic that manages to absorb the difficulty raised by Sunstein's research on "asymmetrical updating." In this way, the essay keeps its eye on the persistent question of how we might preserve the value of evidence-based reasoning even as we recognize its limits in certain contexts.

Adam Sneed

The Conscious and Unconscious Natures of Belief

In "The Ethics of Belief," William Clifford offers an unyielding argument against beliefs formed on the basis of what he believes to be insufficient evidence. He argues that the motivation for the creation of these beliefs, despite the lack of evidence to support them, is "the sense of power attached to a sense of knowledge," something he believes "makes men desirous of believing, and afraid of doubting" (Clifford 34). Clifford is convinced that discovering truths that contradict what we previously believed "leaves us bare and powerless where we thought that we were safe and strong," and because of this people make conscious decisions to reinforce personal convictions rather than challenge them, whether or not their beliefs are erroneous (34). Though he talks about sufficiency throughout his piece, Clifford does not ever indicate what his measure of 'sufficiency' is, nor does he provide anecdotal evidence that illustrates instances where sufficient evidence has been applied to the formation of belief. By building his argument on the instance of belief formation always being a conscious act, Clifford maintains the upper hand, and thus his ability to condemn those who 'chose' to form erroneous beliefs.

Clifford's theory of belief is ambitious in the sense that it assumes people can ignore completely their personal beliefs when analyzing evidence; the idea that people try to adjust their beliefs in response to legitimate evidence, but unconscious biases limit the efficacy of that attempt, is the argument that Cass R. Sunstein makes in "How People Update Beliefs About Climate Change." Sunstein and his associates come to their conclusion by examining the responses of people with differing degrees of belief in climate change when the participants are presented with facts regarding predictions in temperature changes. In their student, the authors polled more than 300 American's responses to various 'news' pieces that either contradicted or confirmed what these people claimed to already believe. This study showcased that confirmation biases—or, an inclination to reaffirm preexisting beliefs—is alive and well in the American population. Strong believers in climate change proved to respond more readily to evidence suggesting that climate change was worse than previously believed. This responsiveness to 'bad news' is illustrated by the proportional increases in what strong climate change believers suspected the temperature change to be in 90 years time. The exact opposite was true when weak climate change believers were given news stories that indicated good things for the planet. Those who were considered weak climate change believers were more likely to be responsive to positive developments, and therefore their predictions for temperature increases were lower than that of the strong climate change believers. According to Sunstein's line of thought, these participants are making an active choice to adjust their predictions based upon the evidence that they have received. In the eyes of these author's, participants are analyzing, to the best of their ability, the evidence that has been presented to them. It is not a lack of trying, but the reality of vastly different sets of foundational beliefs, and "motivated reasoning" which encourages people to place a certain emphasis on "personally relevant" and "affirming" information when considering evidence (Sunstein et al 86). It is these personal motivations and biases which bar the participants from coming to the same conclusions as people with different beliefs and backgrounds, even if two groups were presented with similar evidence. These biases, which the participants are not necessarily conscious of, affect their ability to adjust their beliefs even when presented with legitimate evidence that contradicts what they previously thought to be true. Pre-existing biases lead to what Sunstein calls "asymmetrical updating" (79). An example of asymmetrical updating is showcased by weak climate change believers changing their temperature predictions "far more in response to unexpected good news, suggesting that average temperature rise is likely to be (even) smaller than previously thought," than they were to bad news, which would have challenged their beliefs (76). It is not that these people are not reading statements with both positive and negative outlooks on the future of climate change; it is just that they are simply more inclined to utilize and absorb evidence that confirms what they already believe to be true. The reasons for these fundamental differences in belief systems are not an active choice made by the participants, but rather an unfortunate side effect of living in vastly different environments.

Sunstein accepts that unconscious biases contribute to every individual's decision-making processes; Clifford's theory fails to acknowledge the role of the subconscious and pre-existing beliefs in the decision-making process. In his narrative, Clifford accuses every individual for holding convictions which "instead of being honestly earned by patient inquiring, were stolen by listening to the voice of prejudice and passion" (Clifford 32). This condemnation of people for holding erroneous beliefs is dependent upon the fact that people, when making decisions, have complete agency and are therefore fully conscious of what choices they are making and why. Clifford's idea of complete consciousness comes into play in his essay through the story of the shipowner. Though it had been suggested to a shipowner that his ship might be in need of repair before transporting people across the ocean. Instead of taking action to remedy the problem, the shipowner convinced himself that the ship was seaworthy before leaving the port in order to avoid the discomfort, time and energy it would cost the shipowner if it turned out the ship was not seaworthy and needed to be repaired. Clifford claims that by the shipowner convincing himself of the seaworthiness of the ship despite the questions raised that challenged this belief, the shipowner would subsequently "dismiss from his mind all ungenerous suspicions" and in this way, the shipowner "acquired a sincere and comfortable conviction that his vessel was thoroughly safe and seaworthy" (31). The story ends with the ship's inability to cross the ocean safely and the death of all those aboard. In this scenario, the deaths of those on board can easily be blamed on the negligence of the shipowner. Clifford's theory of belief takes the idea of guilt in a scenario such as this one step further by stating that eve if the ship completed the voyage safely it would not "diminish the guilt of the owner" (31). Clifford's theory claims this is because guilt, which is not dependent upon outcome in Clifford's line of thought, exists not because the conviction of the shipowner was not strong enough, but because "he had no right to believe on such evidence as was before him" (31). The shipowner, by convincing himself so totally of the soundness of the ship without taking into consideration the doubts of those around him, he failed to develop a belief based upon sufficient evidence. In Clifford's theory, this inability to consider all evidence is an active choice made by the shipowner so that he can save himself the inconvenience and discomfort of doubting what he believes to be true. The initial decision to deem the ship seaworthy without gathering sufficient evidence led the shipowner to make subsequent decisions in which he took little notice of proof which contradicted his belief. This proves guilt as well as predicting future behavior. According to Clifford, the lack of legitimate evidence the shipowner considered in this instance will be the way in which he approaches decision and belief-making in the future.

While Clifford is convinced that not considering all evidence with equal weight is a conscious decision, Sunstein's experiment indicated that unconscious biases exist, but individuals attempt to make conscious efforts to consider all evidence when making decisions. Though weak climate change believers were never convinced of the inevitability of a six-degree increase in temperature, there were marginal changes in individuals' predictions of the numerical value of the temperature increase. This showcases the fundamental problem with Clifford's line of thought, which is the fact that he refuses to acknowledge there are outside forces — educational, familial, and other backgrounds — which limit people from being able to remove their personal beliefs from their decision-making process. Clifford does not recognize, or admit, the great personal stake individuals have in what they believe. An example given in Sunstein's piece describes a strong climate change believer who is presented with evidence stating past predictions were incorrect and that, in fact, the planet was much better off than previously thought. On the one hand, this is good news for the planet, but on the other, Sunstein claims this could "suggest that [strong climate change believers had] been wrong to focus on climate change, or to be…alarmed by it" (Sunstein 86). Clifford's argument is unable to account for the "priors," or pre-existing beliefs and experiences, which Sunstein accept as an unavoidable fact in their study (80). The blind-spot created in Clifford's theory of belief, by refusing to acknowledge

pre-existing biases and motivations, is so great that it almost completely prevents it from being useful in the real world. Clifford's condemnation of those who struggle to find truth somewhere in the space between new information and the beliefs they hold paralyzes people from making any decision, or forming any opinion, out of fear that the evidence is insufficient. In this way,
Clifford's theory serves an ideological purpose, forcing every individual to question the legitimacy of his or her beliefs, but practically, is found to be nearly useless.

If Sunstein's study was accepted as the best approach in forming and considering origins of belief, no one would be held accountable for failing to consider all legitimate evidence. If Clifford's theory was accepted in the same way, everyone would be guilty of negligence, and thus be unable to form beliefs based upon sufficient evidence because of the vague nature of the 'sufficiency' marker as well as the human tendency to do what is in one's own best interest.

Together, these two theories present challenges for one another: for Clifford, it is a challenge to be more human and less harsh in his judgment of sufficiency; for Sunstein, it is a challenge to hold people, regardless of belief, to a higher standard, one which forces each individual to consider theories of thought outside their own. Neither is correct or incorrect in its entirety, but by considering these bodies of work alongside one another, a more holistic, or 'sufficient,' theory and real-world practice of belief can be formed.

Works Cited

Clifford, William. "The Ethics of Belief." 1877. Rpt. in *English 125: Academic Writing and The Art of Evidence*. Comp. Adam Sneed, 2016: 31-40. Print.

Sunstein, Cass R. et al. "How People Update Beliefs About Climate Change: Good News and Bad News. Rpt. in *English 125: Academic Writing and The Art of Evidence*. Comp. Adam Sneed, 2016: 78-89. Print.

Music for Non-musicians

Jason Jin
From English 125
Nominated by Aaron Burch

Last semester, for our final essay of the term, I opened up the prompt to allow the specific genre to be of the students' choosing. Rather than looking for essays that met specific goals set forward by myself or a rubric, it forefronted everything we spent the semester talking about—Argument, having a Driving Question for which you are seeking an answer, investigation and curiosity—and so required the students to think about and be aware of their own specific goals while also encouraging creativity. Jason's essay is an exemplar of this creativity, and of self-determined and –guided goals at work.

As we discussed all semester, this essay has at its core a question—"Why did I play clarinet even after I had decided to not pursue music as a career?"—while Jason, as author, and the essay itself, continues to ask smaller and deeper follow-up questions. "Why?" again and again, each microquestion getting closer and closer to helping uncover that big, central question.

It was a manifold pleasure to read. Perhaps first, as a strong essay turned in for class. One that that so admirably exhibits exactly the lessons we spent the semester focusing on, while also finding its own path as means to exhibit those lessons. It shows an embracing of our class goals while also a creativity to get there on its own terms. And finally, purely as a reader.

Aaron Burch

Music for Non-musicians

I don't even want to go into music. Why am I doing this? Dressed in an uncomfortably elaborate tuxedo, bowtie and all, I think this to myself as I check my uniform in the mirror. The outfit I'm wearing is a far cry from my usual sweatshirt, sweatpants and sneakers, and I can feel the one-size-too-small tuxedo shirt's collar tightly grasping my neck. Hot from all the layers and nearly choked, I quickly get into the car with my clarinet in hand. It's nearly an hour drive to Orchestra Hall, and I have to get there early to warm up. Tonight the other members of the Detroit Symphony Orchestra Civic Youth Ensembles (DSO CYE) Philharmonic Orchestra and I are playing *Capriccio espagnol*, a five-movement piece composed by Nikolai Rimsky-Korsakov.

The long drive gives me time to think, or rather, question. I've played clarinet for almost 6 years now, a pretty long time since I picked it up in 6th grade. Within that period, I've done a lot with the instrument, from all-state band to DSO CYE. Yet at some point in high school, I realized I didn't want to pursue music as a profession. Despite the accomplishments I had, I was never really the best player: compared to some of the other players in my ensembles, my high notes were sharp, my articulation was sloppy, and my counting was off. I didn't want to enter into a field in which I was mediocre. Plus, I didn't like the idea of practicing 4 hours a day.

It's been a while since I made the decision not to become a professional musician. Yet here I am, in this cramped tuxedo, driving to a concert. Once again, why am I doing this?

The thought, lingering unfinished, is interrupted by my mom. "We're here!" she announces. As soon as I open the car door, I'm brutally smacked by the cold. I don't mind it too much. Living in Michigan for so long, I'm used to it by now. However, in the interest of protecting my clarinet's wood from cracking, I rush inside. Pulling the large glass doors back, I am greeted by the warmth of indoor heating and the familiar sound of instruments warming up.

After a brief warm-up, the concert organizer notifies us that we should move on-stage. Following the organizer's instructions, we move to our seats in small groups, and as tradition dictates, the first chair violinist comes onto the stage last to tune the entire orchestra. The conductor follows, bows to the audience, and steps onto the podium. The conductor raises his baton, and for a brief moment, there is total silence. I can hear the breaths of the musicians around me. A million eyes are fixed upon the conductor, awaiting his command. With the drop of his baton, sound explodes throughout Orchestra Hall.

Movement I, Alborada, starts with a fantastic flare. Nearly every instrument plays the same rhythm, so loud and grand that I remember jumping out of my seat the first time I listened to it. An exciting dance to celebrate the rising of the sun, the movement is filled with relentless energy, so much so that I can see the violins in front of me sway back and forth with the momentum of the music. Just as quickly as they entered, the notes pull back, and the first clarinet enters in with a brilliant solo. Trills and arpeggios soar through the expansive auditorium.

Assigned the second part for clarinet, I get to watch our principal clarinetist in the spotlight. From the audience's point of view, the solo seems easy. Watch as our first clarinetist boldly and effortlessly sails through the notes! It must be nice to get so much attention for so little work. I too once thought the same; when I first listened to a recording of it, I scoffed at the repetition and simplicity. Yet as I watch her play the solo, I am in awe. I remember my own attempt to play it as a required excerpt for my audition for CYE. I remember not being able to smoothen the C to D trill. I remember not being able to tongue the staccato notes dryly enough. I remember not being able time the fingerings correctly. I remember sitting on the couch, mouth sore, sweaty, frustrated, staring angrily at the measures eluding me. Listening to the pure, unbroken solo, I feel a brief pang of guilt for not being good.

My temporary regret comes to a close as Alborada fades into the second movement, Variazioni. Variazioni is the slow section, basically an obligation in every orchestral piece. Like every other slow section, I switch between a few roles. In the best case, I get to play the boringly easy melody consisting of relatively long notes. Otherwise, I am alternating between the same two slow notes measure after measure, or even worse holding out a long note till I run out of breath.

Variazioni is the other end of the spectrum from the solo in Alborada: it's so easy it hurts. In fact, during rehearsals, I struggled to not fall asleep. I feel like I should hate it for being so unchallenging. After all, I hate other mundane tasks like cleaning my room and making vocab lists. However, in truth, this section is probably the section I enjoy it the most. When I catch myself humming *Capriccio espagnol* on a random day, it's always the French horn part of this movement. Perhaps because it is so simple it is so memorable. Difficulty and beauty aren't mutually inclusive.

Variazioni ends, signaling the beginning of another fast movement: Alborada. If that title seems familiar, it's because it's the same as the first movement. In fact, the melody and tempo are the same; the only differences are that it's shorter and there's no clarinet solo, instead a violin one.

Despite the unoriginality, this movement evokes an important idea: repetition. As we experience life, we come across common ideas. My ponderings in the first two movements reappear in many other contexts within my life. The perception of incompetence isn't limited to just music. When I see the first clarinetist's face, I actually see many more. I see the faces of those who beat me in chess tournaments when I was in elementary school, satisfied after taking advantage of a foolish blunder I made in hubris. I see the faces of those who beat me in tennis tournaments, sweaty after two excruciating hours of running and hitting. I see the faces those who scored higher than I in Michigan Math Prize Competition, smiling for the camera as they collected awards for places above mine. Every time, I am overcome with a temporary wave of frustration and jealousy, quelled by a motivation to be better.

The second movement's message too replays throughout my life. It manifests in the form of the small satisfactions. Even with the most common and trivial tasks, I am rewarded with a sense of accomplishment. When I finish writing my vocab lists for Spanish, despite understanding that almost anyone else could have done the same thing, I feel a bit of pride. When I organize my binder of notes and assignments, despite knowing that it's nothing special, I get a small surge of confidence. The envy from difficulty and the satisfaction from easiness, they recur time and time again. Repetitions like these make life manageable, and in a way knowing that some things, like the warmth of family and friends, will always be there is beautiful, like the images of a kaleidoscope.

As Alborada fades away for the second and final time, we are greeted by a piercing drum roll. The fourth movement, Scena e canto gitano, has arrived. The hall is decorated with solo after solo: a trumpet solo, then a violin solo, then a clarinet solo, then an oboe solo, then a harp solo. Done successively and separately, they foster a deep appreciation of the individual sound of each instrument. As the orchestra comes to play together once again, I'm met with a sudden awareness of each instrument's contribution to the orchestra as a whole.

Scena e canto gitano reminds me of the idea of diversity. From a very young age, we are constantly hammered with the idea that diversity is great. Even on the bus today, I look up and behold a message from the University of Michigan. In big bold letters, it says "enrage," but the r is crossed out to instead spell "engage." Signs like these exemplify that we are often commanded to treasure diversity without being shown or told why. Listening to the magnificent music in the air, each instrument building off of each other to craft an otherwise unobtainable sound, I understand from personal experience that there is beauty in diversity, there is harmony in difference.

It is more than diversity between people; it is also diversity within oneself. Bringing in and considering diverse ideas enriches the experience of life. Taking in the frustration from the first movement and the appreciation from the second, I am both confident because of all that I can already do and motivated because of all that I want to be able to do. A fulfilling life is one guided by more than just a singular principle, but instead a shifting collection of diverse ideas.

The final movement, Fandango asturiano, start seamlessly from the fourth; there is no break of silence in between them. As the movement progresses, the tempo accelerates, becoming more frantic and raw until finally, on the last line, we repeat the same melody from the first movement, louder and faster and wilder than ever before. Despite how tired I am, the fandango, so ceaselessly and unapologetically happy, reminds me of how I want to live my life: not perpetually joyful, that would be unhealthy, but consistently and profoundly happy. It's a difficult thing to achieve, but it's possible through the lessons of the previous movements. Putting all of our breath into one final push, the orchestra ends with a chord that rattles the entire hall. Sweaty and out of breath, I smile as the audience stands up and responds with thunderous applause.

Why do I play music? Part of it is that I enjoy classical music. But if that was the only reason, I would just be a listener. No, for me, music has a greater meaning. It touches upon ideas that I don't encounter in everyday life. When I'm doing homework, I don't really think about whether I'm happy and how I'll be happy, but these thoughts come up all the time when I'm playing music. Music has a lot of important things to say, about happiness, about life, about whatever you interpret it to be about. However, you learn the most from music when you play, rather than listen to, music.

The Complexity of Grief

Jaylin Herskovitz
From English 125
Nominated by Tiffany Ball

Jaylin Herskovitz's essay, "The Complexity of Grief," offers a research-based analysis of the "ambiguous grief" at the center of Alison Bechdel's graphic narrative *Fun Home*. The essay contextualizes its reading of Fun Home through meticulous, interdisciplinary research into the cultural history of mourning and psychological studies of the grieving process. Attending simultaneously to the novel's formal qualities and its historical context, Jaylin argues that Bechdel's "cycles of analysis and mediation" are best understood through examples of modern grief theory that depart from the goal of attaining closure to focus on the ways in which one can manage and live with loss. Overall, this essay is both a compelling piece of literary criticism and an insightful meditation on how to grieve for a complicated person.

For this research assignment, students were required to incorporate three scholarly sources into their essays, but Jaylin's lengthy bibliography testifies to the fact that she is a student who surpasses expectations and requirements. Jaylin doesn't just want to complete an assignment; she wants to solve a puzzle. One of the things that I tell my students about inquiry-driven research is that good research can be unsettling. You begin researching a topic and, through a series of twists and turns, end up somewhere you didn't think you'd be. As a researcher and writer, Jaylin is tenacious and open to following new lines of inquiry. She's willing to sit with that feeling of being unmoored, and this essay is a testament to the payoffs of doing so.

Tiffany Ball

The Complexity of Grief

Grief is very obviously a complicated emotion. The question of how and why we grieve has been asked over and over, with answers changing over time. In this essay, I first want to give a brief history and interpretation of bereavement theory. I'd then like to discuss Alison Bechdel's graphic memoir *Fun Home* within the historical context of these theories. *Fun Home* is an embodiment of Bechdel's personal coping experience, and is an example of how even those that have their views of grief shaped by outdated ideas can overcome them and find peace. Bechdel's novel works to subvert expectations of mourning and closure in popular culture and ultimately present a modern view of what grief can be.

Humanity has dealt with death and loss since its beginnings, but the ways that this has been done have varied greatly. Before the twentieth century, ritualistic and social mourning was prevalent. In an overview of the evolution of grief theory, Megan O'Rourke writes that "to lose someone was once to be swept into a flurry of rituals". Practices were incredibly restrictive as well. For example, in England and the United States during the Victorian era, mourners applied rules to their social lives and followed strict dress codes: female mourners were only permitted to wear "stiff black crêpes", and only after some time could add gray and lavender to their wardrobe (O'Rourke). Jewish mourners perform shivah, a period that usually lasts seven days, to honor those who have passed by stopping their everyday routines completely. Strict observers are not permitted to "enjoy the sound of music, or any other forms of amusement" during this time, nor can they attend "joyous events" for a period of thirty days ("The Shiva and Other Mourning Observances"). O'Rourke also writes that Hindus "visit the house of the bereaved for twelve days and chant hymns". These rituals characterize grief as an activity of the community, but something that also has a definite and prescribed end.

Entering into the twentieth century, the story of bereavement theory in western culture, like most other areas of psychoanalysis, begins with Freud.

Many of his ideas have lingered, perhaps the most important being the idea of "grief work" as a whole. This concept, proposed in 1917, that "people whose loved ones had died needed to work through the loss", that grief and emotional trauma needed attention and time to heal, has lived on, and theorists still build on the idea that grief is a process (Rothaupt 6). But, Freud's end goal for grief was complete emotional detachment. As before, there was a finite end to mourning. Freud's theories also coincide with a shift in the public view of grief. Both the Civil War and World War I created "ambiguous loss", as Pauline Boss and Donna Carnes put it in their essay "The Myth of Closure". Religious rituals had already been falling out of fashion, and because in many cases the bereaved families did not have a body to bury, they could not turn to the traditional funeral. In a stereotypical American fashion, we buried these painful emotions, "we [denied] death and [insisted] on the tidiness of closure" (Boss 4). Boss and Carnes claim that the "cultural legacy" of the United States is wrapped up in denying our own need to mourn, in a "massive unresolved loss" (Boss 4). Around this time, Freud writes *Mourning and Melancholia*, and, as O'Rourke puts it, "In a stroke, the work of mourning had become internalized", as he defined grief "as something fundamentally private and individual" (O'Rourke). This idea that grief is an emotion that a single person must process until they reach a point of closure has unfortunately remained in the public mind. Closure gained more and more popularity with the work of Elisabeth Kübler-Ross, who first introduced the five stage model for grief. These stages "pervade pop culture", showing up in television programs, movies, and books (O'Rourke). At the time that her work was introduced, it signified a large change—talking openly about death and dying was still largely avoided. But even though her method had a different end-goal than Freud's did (acceptance), the notion of having an end-goal at all was still there. O'Rourke suggests that her work gained popularity because "it made loss sound controllable", a complex emotion packaged into five neat steps.

Grief theory has come a long way since then, and the idea of closure has faded among scholars. Worden's "task model" for grief, presented in 1991, involved goals for patients that could be completed in any order and revisited later on. Although this was more fluid, it still had the goal of 'letting go' of the deceased (Rothaupt 8). In 2004, Walsh and McGoldrick advised open communication and expression of feelings, and instead of the concrete idea of complete closure, presented the idea of "adapting" to the loss and reaching a new "equilibrium" in one's life (Rothaupt 8). The language regarding grief work began to change as well: words like "manage" and "adapt" began to replace ones like "recover" (Rothaupt 8). Boss and Carnes propose a new goal for grief work, and that is "to live with grief by finding meaning", which is representative of the shift in ideas in the field as a whole.

However, the negative effects of the popularization of the work of Freud and Kübler-Ross live on in mainstream ideas. Nancy Berns introduces the idea of "closure marketing" in her essay "Chasing Closure". She gives the examples of the funeral and death care industry, which advertise their services as necessary to providing closure, and death penalty advocates claiming that it would be a method to bring closure to victim's families (Berns 51). In both of these cases, there are still people who cannot achieve closure, and thus are left feeling "abnormal, complicated, or chronic" (Berns 53). Berns argues that it is the "distorted understanding" of grief that leads to emotional distress when it does not come perfectly. Boss and Carnes even state that closure can be an "unhealthy goal" because it is sometimes impossible, especially in ambiguous cases (Boss 2).

Alison Bechdel's loss of her father is one such ambiguous case. In *Fun Home*, Bechdel presents a vision of grief muddled with conflicting troublesome relationships and conflicting emotions. *Fun Home* is filled with opposing themes. It explores a multitude of oppositions: appearances and inner truth, masculinity and femininity, youth and adulthood. Bruce Bechdel, Alison's father, is especially contradictory in his identity and actions, the most obvious discrepancy being the 'open secret' of his sexuality. Every set of opposing ideas seems to join together in Bruce. He is both masculine and feminine, passive and controlling, aggressive and caring. Alison cannot explain or comprehend the contradictions that exist in her father, and thus cannot explain his death, which she believes to be a suicide. She has an initial goal of reaching closure, stemming from ideas present in her childhood home. Growing up helping around her family's funeral home, Alison quickly becomes aware that people hold funerals for themselves, to mourn and move on. Combine this idea with her mother and father's lack of emotion and communication, and she has a perfect recipe for Freudian style grieving: closure focused and alone. However, her lack of a deep sadness for her father makes this process more complex. These complications drive Alison to find less traditional methods of grieving and unraveling the clashing feelings that she has for him.

In the beginning, Alison attempts to use a variety of methods to grieve, in addition to the interpretation of literature. She utilizes photographs alongside an analysis of Proust's novel *Remembrance of Things Past* to further show the contradictions that her father embodies, analyzing the novel while also showing photographs and scenes of her father while on a family vacation. She explains a the metaphor of two different paths in *A Remembrance of Things Past*, that they are "initially presented as diametrically opposed", that they represent "bourgeois versus aristocratic, homo versus hetero, city versus country, eros versus art, private versus public" (102). Bruce seems to represent many of these. The lifestyle he leads, which is focused on art, literature, and appearances, is at odds with his sexual desires – eros. He enjoys the city and its romantic nature – Alison even wonders if her father's love for her mother came from a love from her surroundings, New York City (105) – while also being attached to nature, growing up on a farm, and living his whole life in a small city. His sexuality is public and private at the same time; outwardly he is heterosexual, but his closeted sexuality still manages to present itself. Alongside this, Alison shows a strip of negatives from their family vacation. The first few are bright shots of her and her brothers on the beach, while the last one is a darker, erotic photograph of a young man who babysat for them, Roy. These photographs illustrate Bruce's contrasting desires, one to have a family and keep up appearances, and the other to engage sexually with young men. And although he tried to keep the latter a secret, the fact that Alison has found these photographs anyways after his death shows his inability to keep it truly hidden from his family. Continuing her analysis of Proust's work, Alison writes "But at the end of the novel the two ways are revealed to converge – to have always converged" (102). Just as the two paths are one and the same, so do these contradictory ideas merge inside of Bruce, and Bechdel brings multiple sources into play to show this.

Alison analyzes her father's life in the same way that she analyzes literature. On page 120, Alison holds two photographs, one in each hand, the left a photograph of Bruce from his college fraternity, sunbathing on a roof, the right a picture of herself smiling on a fire escape. The fact that Alison is looking at these photographs alone is telling of the distant relationship between her and Bruce. Usually, parents will share memories with their children or flip through photo albums together. Alison's attempts to learn about her father's life without him is a stark contrast to the norm, but emphasizes her desire to know more about what was going through her father's mind at the time. Like analyzing details from a novel, she notes the physical similarities between the two of them: "the exterior setting, the painted grin, the flexible wrists, even the angle of shadow falling across our faces" (120). She begins to speculate, wondering if the boy who took her father's photograph was his lover simply because the girl that took her photograph was hers. This is Alison's thesis: she assumes that her father's happiness comes from being open about his sexuality, that his experiences of coming out or experimenting sexually match her own. But, there isn't much basis for this aside from the fact that her father had sexual relationships with younger men – she doesn't know if he openly had boyfriends or even if he felt the desire to. And yet, Alison still tries to make some connection and figure out the reasoning behind his choices and suicide.

Alison's use of photographs in her grieving is important because it further illustrates her desire for control over the mourning process. In an essay from the International Journal of Play Therapy, an essay entitled "Play Therapy and Photo-Elicitation: A Narrative Examination of Children's Grief" explains how photography can be integrated into children's therapy. Since "children have not developed the complex, expressive language skills to explain their emotions in relation to a loss", photo-elicitation (or the act of taking photographs) is used to give them a sense of control in how they express their loss (Stutey 2). And although Alison isn't the one taking the photographs that she examines, she alone has the power to interpret them. This power is important—Alison's expectations of grief haven't been fulfilled, which leaves her feeling helpless. Even the novel as a whole represents a desire for control: she outs her father as homosexual and portrays her family as she chooses. But, Alison only has this desire because the goal of closure has left her unable to process her emotions, grasping at straws and trying to make sense of an ambiguous loss.

Obviously, this method of photographic analysis is somewhat futile and doesn't allow Alison to reach a closing point. In another scene of photographic analysis, Alison closely examines the erotic photo of Roy that was found in an envelope with other photos from the trip. She wonders "Why, for that matter, leave the photo in the envelope at all?" (101). However, the only conclusion that she reaches at this point is to confirm more contradictory behavior, saying the feeble attempt to hide the photo is "An act of prestidigitation typical of the way my father juggled his public appearance and private reality" and that "the evidence is simultaneously hidden and revealed" (101), emphasizing the 'open secret' in Bruce's life and how his sexuality is both public and private. She is unable to understand the reasoning behind his actions and why he chose to keep his sexuality a secret, and thus is stuck attempting to make sense of what she is left with.

At this point, one wonders why Alison chooses to analyze her father's life in this way at all. The process of examining literature is meant to be subjective, emotionless. But because she has to parse all of the complexities intertwined in her attachment to her father, she is left to find alternate methods to use to move on. It seems odd that Alison would apply the same techniques – inspecting photographs and creating parallels between her father and *A Remembrance of Things Past* – to her relationship with her father and his death, which is usually an emotional experience. Though, Alison's experience with her father's death is anything but traditional. In one scene, she laughs while telling a friend about her father's death (227). In another, after hearing that her father had had sexual relationships with young men, she says the news left her stupefied "but not quite stupefied enough", and she "remedies this condition" by getting high (79). At her father's funeral, she wishes "If only they made smelling salts to induce grief-stricken swoons rather than snap you out of them" (52). She recognizes here that something is definitely wrong with her emotionless experience; she even desires to feel grief and sadness. Why though would Alison choose to put herself through the process of analyzing her father's suicide? Why is she unable to continue on normally with her life, even though her father was such a large destructive force in her life?

Alison's strategy and process of doing this enables her to cycle through her relationship with her father and to work through the issues that they had in their relationship. It is clear that Bruce is a difficult person to grieve for. At the end of the fourth chapter, after recalling a camping trip with her father where her and her brothers had seen a snake, she discusses the serpent as a symbol, writing "It's obviously a phallus, yet a more ancient and universal symbol of the feminine principle would be hard to come by" (116). Here she alludes to the biblical story of Adam and Eve, where Eve is tempted by a serpent to sin. Bechdel claims that the snake represents a contradiction, embodying both the masculine and feminine, that serpents have a "nonduality" (116). She then goes on to state "Maybe that's what's so unsettling about snakes. They also imply a cyclicality, life from death" (116). Earlier in the chapter, Alison confirms that her father embodies all sorts of contradictions, and now, she makes the connection between contradictions and their unsettling nature. Alison is personally unsettled by her father's choices because the things that he does seem to oppose one another, and she cannot derive his reasoning from this. The connection is then made between contradictions and cyclicality. Alison is absolutely trapped in a cycle of analysis because she is trying to reach closure when faced with Bruce's idiosyncrasies. Her emotional trauma isn't solved in a way that is expected, but the procedure that she turns to allows her to progress. In addition, and as a whole, *Fun Home* is incredibly cyclical. Each chapter goes over different memories, just as chapter four does, and looks at Bruce's suicide in a new light. *Fun Home* itself is a manifestation of Bechdel's cycles of recovery; it is an artifact of her process of grieving. After living through dealing with her own emotions by connecting them to secondary sources, Bechdel writing this novel is another method of mediating her feelings through literature, but this time it is her own.

Boss and Carnes introduce this same idea of embracing contradictions in loss as a method of understanding an ambiguous loss. They claim that in the case of "paradoxical loss", seemingly contradictory thoughts are the "most authentic way to think" (Boss 9). To force oneself to only believe one side of contradictory thought would be to erase the other. They give a few example phrases that a patient might try to embrace: "My loved one is both gone— and still here; I am both my mother's child—and now the mother of my mother; I am both married—and a widow(er) waiting to happen" (Boss 9). Boss and Carnes also state that "grief is an oscillating process of ups and downs" (Boss 7). This further emphasizes how *Fun Home* is an embodiment of modern grief theory.

Each of Alison's cycles of analysis – calling up old memories, reviewing photographs, and making connections to works of literature – is a form of mediation for dealing with this cycle. At the end of chapter four, Alison notes that after her father died "an updated translation of Proust came out. *Remembrance of Things Past* was re-titled *In Search of Lost Time*" and says "The new title is a more literal translation of *A la Recherché du Temps Perdu*, but it still doesn't quite capture the full resonance of *perdu*. This means not just lost but ruined, undone, wrecked, and spoiled" (119). Where before, Alison used Proust's work to analyze her father, she now uses it to explain her own emotions and reasoning. If she can't show any sort of remorse for her father's death, it minimizes any positive memories she has with him, and it 'undoes' their relationship. Even in the first chapter, Alison says that after he has died "his absence resonated retroactively, echoing back through all the time I knew him" (23). Accompanying this are images of positive memories she has with him: mowing the lawn together and taking a bath. These small slices of good in their relationship are what Alison is hanging onto and what she doesn't want to lose, despite all of the awful things that her father has done in her life as well, a contradiction in itself. Because their relationship was so far from the norm, to be completely passive about his death would be to limit it, and to take away the incongruities in it. About the translation of perdu, she writes: "What's lost in translation is the complexity of loss itself" (120), and Alison's emotions on the loss of her father truly are complex.

Bechdel's cycles of analysis and mediation allow herself to accept all of these complexities, to feel conflicting emotions and to embrace them, even with her strange methods of doing so. In any situation, grief and feelings of sadness and loss and despair are always mediated. But, *Fun Home* represents a shift away from traditional forms of mediation (i.e. the funeral) and towards new ones. It is true that Alison's mediation of her feelings using analysis of secondary sources is complex. But, grief as a whole is a complex emotion and thus, how it should be processed will be complicated as well. Attempting to simplify this process only results in frustration. Like all other emotions, grief cannot be flattened, and *Fun Home* presents a well-rounded view of mourning that aligns with contemporary theories, showing readers each facet of a complete and modern grief experience.

Works Cited

Bechdel, Alison. *Fun Home: A Family Tragicomic*. Boston: Houghton Mifflin, 2006. Print.

Berns, Nancy. "Chasing "Closure"." *Contexts* Fall 2011: 48-53. *ProQuest*. Web. 6 Apr. 2016.

Boss, Pauline, and Donna Carnes. "The Myth of Closure." *Family Process* 51.4 (2012): 456- 469. *PsycINFO*. Web. 6 Apr. 2016.

Cvetkovich, Ann. "Drawing the Archive in Alison Bechdel's Fun Home." *WSQ: Women's Studies Quarterly* 36.1 & 2 (2008): 111-28. *Project MUSE.* Project MUSE. Web. 7 Apr. 2016.

DeGroot, M.H., J. de Keijser, and J. Neeleman. "Grief Shortly After Suicide and Natural Death: A Comparative Study among Spouses and First-Degree Relatives." *Suicide & Life - Threatening Behavior* 36.4 (2006): 418-31. *ProQuest.* Web. 6 Apr. 2016.

Gall, Terry Lynn, Jesse Henneberry, and Melissa Eyre. "Two Perspectives on the Needs of Individuals Bereaved By Suicide." *Death Studies* 38.7 (2014): 430-437. *PsycINFO.* Web. 6 Apr. 2016.

O'Rourke, Meghan. "Good Grief." Editorial. *New Yorker* 1 Feb. 2010: n. pag. *The New Yorker.* Condé Nast. Web. 10 Apr. 2016.

Rothaupt, Jeanne W. "A Literature Review of Western Bereavement Theory: From Decathecting to Continuing Bonds." *The Family Journal: Counseling and Therapy for Couples and Families* 15 (2007): 6-15. *SAGE Journals.* Web. 10 Apr. 2016.

Stutey, Diane M., et al. "Play Therapy and Photo-Elicitation: A Narrative Examination of Children's Grief." *International Journal of Play Therapy* (2015): *PsycINFO.* Web. 6 Apr. 2016.

"The Basics—The Shiva and Other Mourning Observances." *Chabad.* Chabad. org, n.d. Web. 13 Apr. 2016.

Wojtkowiak, Joanna, M.Sc, Verena Wild M.Sc, and Jos Egger PhD. "Grief Experiences and Expectance of Suicide." *Suicide & Life - Threatening Behavior* 42.1 (2012): 56. *ProQuest.* Web. 6 Apr. 2016.

Matt Kelley/Granader Family Prize for Excellence in First-Year Writing

On behalf of the Sweetland Center for Writing I am delighted to introduce and congratulate Stephanie Bloom and Miles Honey, winners of the Granader Family Prize for Outstanding Writing Portfolio; Xiowei Ou and Fengyi Tong, winners the Granader Family Award for Excellence in Multilingual Writing; and Serena Scholz and Bailey Stein, winners of the Matt Kelley/ Granader Family Award for Excellence in First-Year Writing. These students' work impressed this year's judges with the unexpected ways students answered the challenges their first-year courses posed for them. Our award winners found creative, innovative ways to build arguments and explore questions about advertising, chemistry, astronomy, texting, grief, and chance. Their writing is thoughtful, engaging, and a genuine pleasure to read.

Instructors also deserve congratulations and thanks for the work you see here. They carefully construct courses, craft writing assignments, recognize good student writing when they see it, and share the wealth with us by nominating their students. I am grateful to my colleagues in the Sweetland Center for Writing who served as judges for this year's writing prizes: Paul Barron, Scott Beal, Gina Brandolino, Louis Cicciarelli, T Hetzel, Lillian Li, Shelley Manis, Christine Modey, Simone Sessolo, and Naomi Silver. I am especially grateful to Raymond McDaniel and Carol Tell, who volunteered to serve as members of the writing prize committee and graciously accepted extra reading. These beautiful volumes would not be possible without the stalwart work of Laura Schuyler and Aaron Valdez, who guide the writing prizes from beginning to end. Finally, I offer my heartfelt thanks to the Granader Family, whose generosity supports the writing prizes. We hope you enjoy these essays as much as we did, and are inspired by the excellent work these talented first-year students have created.

Dana Nichols
Sweetland Center for Writing

The Helsinki Waste Closet Incident

Serena Scholz
From LHSP 125
Nominated by Louis Cicciarelli

As a reader, I was taken by Ms. Scholz's quiet, observant voice in this essay and the skill in her writing. She tells the story of a mother and daughter trip to Finland that is changed when a sister-aunt back at home passes away. Her writing has heart, wit, affection, and specificity of place, and portrays the peculiar feeling of being stuck abroad, trapped on holiday, as events unfold back home, and mother and daughter reckon with their grief. Ms. Scholz's writing conveys the strangeness and beauty of their time in Helsinki on this bittersweet occasion, and in this case, how the minor frustrations of travel can become more resonant as mother and daughter together find a way to carry on.

Louis Cicciarelli

The Helsinki Waste Closet Incident

I awoke to the sound of crying. It was my mom, outside on the balcony. The sound wafted in through the small window, settling over me as I lay in bed. I clung to sleep for a moment before giving up and looking around, dazed. It was half-dark outside, but I didn't know if it was late evening or early morning. My internal clock had been broken by the quick succession of international flights. Around me, the unfamiliar apartment loomed cold and large. I lay in bed for a moment, sad and tired.

I knew what she was crying about. My aunt Margo had died. It didn't come as a surprise to me - she'd been in and out of the hospital for years, so close to death so often that the initial shock had softened, faded into normality. When I was twelve, I fell asleep in math class after a late night drive home from the hospital to say goodbye to her. Now I'm eighteen. It's been six years. We'd just landed in Helsinki, Finland, when my mom got a phone call: Margo was in the hospital again. There was no news for a long time as we waited in a softly lit airport café, sipping coffee and trying to stay awake after our overnight flight from Iceland. It was night back home, and everyone was asleep.

We eventually made our way to a strange apartment complex on the outskirts of Helsinki. It was gray and blocky and modern, all glass and confusing parallel hallways. There were no doorknobs on any of the doors, only a small black keyhole, and after inserting the key into the lock, you simply pulled the door open with the key. Inside was a second, unlocked door, able to be opened with its small handle. The hallways smelled like bleach and boiled cabbage. It was all cold and austere, and our Airbnb host's apartment was no better, decorated in a combination of stainless steel and green glass. I tried to stay awake to adjust to the time zone, but eventually I couldn't hold my eyelids open anymore and I dozed off.

I got out of bed, rubbing my eyes and swaying a bit. The clock on the wall in the kitchen said nine. Whether it was a.m. or p.m. was anyone's guess. I listened to the soft sobs from outside on the balcony, deciding to let her grieve for her sister alone for a moment. The half-darkness made me feel like I was still asleep, in a gray dreamland from which I couldn't awake.

I switched on the lights in the kitchen, but they were dim and didn't help much. I searched through the kitchen cupboards systematically, looking for a tea kettle. Eventually I found one – bright stainless steel and barely used. I filled it with tap water and set it on the stove to boil while I searched through our luggage for our stash of teabags. After finding them, I sat down on the light green couch and waited for the water to boil. The couch was the color of dentist's gloves. The material was cold and glossy, and my legs slid away from me disconcertingly when I tried to curl up.

I made the tea and carried the mugs precariously to the balcony door, opening it with my pinky finger. My mom looked up me. "They decided to pull the plug," she said, eyes red. "They all visited her already. All my sibs. And here I am. In fucking Helsinki!"

I handed her the mug of tea and sat next to her on the porch swing, head on her shoulder. We sat silent for a moment. "What day is it?" I asked finally.

Our time in Helsinki took on a tone of gray. My mom wanted to leave. "It will always be the place where my sister died," she told the airline staff over telephone, as we sat together on the slippery couch.

"Are you going to the funeral?" The voice asked on the other end.

"No," she said, not saying what was at the forefront of both of our minds. *If we leave, we'll never be able to afford to come back.* We'd saved for this trip since I was thirteen. "I just want to change our flight to Iceland to an earlier time. So we can have some more time there." I was happy in Iceland. *Everything here is cold and distant and horrible. Let's leave.*

"I'm sorry ma'am, I'm afraid we can't change your tickets just because you are sad."

There was silence for a moment.

"For $1300 US a seat, we could bump you to an earlier flight, a few days from now-"

My mom hung up the phone. "We're staying."

The next day, we ventured into the city to find Temppeliaukio "Rock" Church. It was a beautiful building, built into dark, solid stone, yet with light airy wooden beams across the glass ceiling. "Not because Margo was religious," my mom clarified, carefully lighting a tealight and placing it in a crevice in the stone wall before turning her face upwards to look at the sky. "Because it's the Rock Church. And Margo loved rock and the blues."

We drifted down the items on our list, only doing the ones we felt most strongly about. "The seaside park," my mom said. "Because Margo loved the big water." Sitting on the sun-warmed stones, we looked out over the many small islands making up Helsinki's archipelago. That was the day my aunt's ashes were to be scattered on the shoreline of Lake Huron, where she'd lived for the past thirty years. "It's all one big water," my mom said into the breeze. I took a picture of her looking out to sea on my phone, and she sent it to her siblings. They all agreed – sitting in the sun and looking out over the quiet waves was the best way to honor her.

Our trip evolved in the roundabout way that unplanned trips do – we'd go somewhere on our list, then wander around under the cloudy skies for a while, eventually ending up somewhere else entirely. One day we ended up caught in the middle of the largest gay pride parade ever organized in Europe. Marchers surged down the major artery of the city, a wave of rainbow blood pouring down the road. The only way to cross and get back home was to join in, which we did. We were carried halfway out of town before washing up on the other side of the street near our apartment complex. That was the first time in days I'd seen my mom truly smile – and I think it was the point when we began to realize that the city of Helsinki – so gray, foreboding, and distant at first glance – was beautiful in its own way.

No matter what we did, we always ended up drifting into bed after we finished our scraped together meals. After our desperate first night's meal out amounted to a $70 bill for two subpar burgers, we'd quickly learned that it was much too expensive to go to restaurants. The supermarket in the basement of our apartment building was much more reasonably priced. For breakfasts, we ate vanilla skyr sprinkled with bright red raspberries, magenta juices staining the white yogurt pink. Despite being used to fresh, homegrown berries from our garden at home, we'd never tasted anything like the delicate sweetness of these Helsinki berries. They melted in your mouth like candy. The first time we ate them, I suspiciously looked at the ingredient list, wondering what the Finnish word for 'sugar' was. I found only *vadelmat* – raspberries. Since then, I've never encountered another berry like the ones we bought in cheap plastic containers from the S-Mart in the basement of that apartment complex.

Sometimes it was difficult to wake up. Despite my valiant efforts to get us out into the sunlight, we both did a lot of sleeping and dreaming, lying in bed in the twilight haze of nighttime at high latitudes. The sun never went fully down, but the world did turn gray and blue for long periods of time. We halfheartedly playing backgammon in bed at night, and later, the silence often gave rise to grief and tears. Our time in Helsinki was surreally beautiful, with the fairytale vistas of island-hopping by day, and our quiet companionship in the half-darkness by night.

On one of our last days staying in the apartment, we decided that we really needed to take out the trash. We'd been avoiding it for too long – tying up bags of food waste and sticking them in the stainless-steel freezer to keep them from smelling – because we couldn't figure out where to take it. My mom finally sent a message to our Airbnb host to ask about it.

"Hi Vadim! Where should we take the garbage to?"

Two hours later, this was the message she received in reply:

"Hello Mary. Thank you for being so kind to take out garbage! I hope you are having a nice stay. To take out the garbage, follow these instructions. Go out the apartment door and turn right. Turn right again down the hallway with the glass door. Go out into the inner courtyard. Turn left and follow the brick wall. Turn right. Follow the wall to the end, there will be an unmarked gray door with small keypad. The code is 1194372. Thank you!"

The instructions seemed a little complicated – we laughed a little at the sheer length of the text message. It was dusk, and we'd just drawn the gauzy curtains closed and turned the dim lamps. Putting our shoes and coats on, we headed out the doorknob-less apartment door into the maze of hallways, each carrying a bag of trash. We followed along with the instructions, point by point.

"Which hallway with the glass door?" My mom wondered out loud as she peeked around a corner. "The first one we passed? Or this one?"

We stood together and looked down our second hallway possibility, which seemed completely identical to the first. The glass door at the end glowed with the last remaining bits of sunlight.

"The one leading into the inner courtyard?" I asked. "So, this one? Or did the other one also lead outside?"

"I don't think so. Let's go this way."

The glass door in question was locked. There was, of course, no doorknob or handle. Eventually we located a small, singular key hole, but our apartment key didn't fit. We turned around and went the other way, fumbling through the quiet hallways with our bags of trash.

We made it outside into what we presumed was the inner courtyard – the small paved area we could see from the apartment balcony where we'd sat together the first night. Turning left, as per the instructions, we looked for a brick wall to follow. The only wall in sight was gray stone of the building. "Mistranslation?" I wondered. My mom shrugged. We walked along it anyways, not knowing what else to do. The dusk grew heavier around us as we tentatively turned right, looking for a gray door amidst the twilight.

"Could this be it?" I leaned down towards a keypad on a dark gray door, squinting a little to read the numbers. I was vaguely pleased to discover that this door actually had a doorknob.

My mom shrugged, unsure. "I hope so. Want me to read you the code?"

"Yeah."

I pressed each button firmly and carefully. *1, 1, 9, 4, 3, 7, 2.* "That's it," said my mom as we reached the last few digits.

I tried the door. Nothing. It wiggled up and down a little, but wouldn't turn.

"Maybe I put the numbers in wrong. Read them to me again?"

I punched in the code again, bare fingers getting a little cold. Scandinavian summer nights were chilly. *3, 7, 2.* I rattled the doorknob, pulling really hard in case it needed more force to open. Nothing. My mom dropped her bag of trash on the ground, sighing and looking around at the empty stone courtyard. "Is there another door?"

I left the trash bag on the ground and wandered up and down the area a little bit, looking around. "No, there's nothing else."

"Ok, let me try. Read me the code."

I took the phone. "1, 1, 9, 4, 3, 7, 2." My mom typed them in one by one then grabbed at the handle and pulled. The door stayed firmly locked. I started to laugh a little bit. "This is ridiculous. Why is taking out the trash so fucking complicated?" She punched in the code again. Still nothing. We stood there in the half-dark, holding our bags of trash, starting to laugh a little bit at our situation.

"Let's go back inside," my mom suggested tiredly, around. "It's getting chilly and we're obviously doing something wrong. We'll read over the instructions again and try again in a bit."

We backtracked to the apartment and sprawled on the bed, pouring over the message and letting our fingers warm up a bit. "Did that, did that, did that, found the door..." But there was little room for misinterpretation in the instructions we'd received. My mom sent Vadim a message back: "Is it possible the code for the door has changed?" He responded promptly. "No, the door code never changes. The code I gave you is correct." My mom looked at me. After about 10 minutes had passed, we got up again. We put on our coats and shoes, double checking we had the apartment key. This time we knew where we were going, and walked directly to the door.

I feigned confidence and walked up to the keypad, typing in the code which I had now memorized from repeated use. I finished and gave the door handle a solid pull, confident it would slide open. It didn't. It stayed locked shut. I jiggled it more, annoyed. My mom started to laugh, and I chuckled a bit.

Hopelessly, I punched in the code again. Still nothing. "We just need to take out the trash!" I said as heaves of laughter began coming out of my chest. My mom was doubled over from laughter. "What the fuck is with this place?" She said, holding her stomach and laughing. We erupted in hysterics in the quiet courtyard, dropping our trash bags again. I was laughing so hard that I couldn't breathe. Every laugh hurt my stomach, but I couldn't stop. I bent over at the waist, unable to stand upright. Tears rolled down my mom's face as she crouched against the gray stone wall. We looked at each other, but that only made us laugh more. *What the hell is going on? Why isn't anything working? Why can't we stop laughing?* I was crying as I punched in the code again. I threw my body weight into pulling the doorknob, but was only rewarded by a strained shoulder. The door stayed firmly in place. I tried to compose myself. My stomach ached and tears were rolling down my cheeks. The gray dusk enveloped us as I sank down next to my mom on the wall opposite the door. I closed my eyes, still shaking and convulsing. I wasn't sure if it was from laughter or sobs. I put my head in my mom's lap. She was crying, chest heaving. I heard the trash bag next to us fall over onto its side.

Some time later, seconds or hours, I opened my eyes and wiped them, looking around. It was still night-dusk outside, but I could see easier than before. The tears had cleaned my eyes out. We stood unsteadily and slowly picked up the trash bags. The breeze in the courtyard was cold and refreshing as it whipped at my raw eyes. Walking back through the glass door, we entered the familiar hallways and let ourselves back into the apartment. Kicking off my shoes, I dropped the trash bags by the door and lay down on the soft bed.

"What do we do with the trash?" I asked after a second.

"I don't know," my mom replied, putting her head on the pillow. "I don't know. Let's just stick it back in the freezer for now, so it doesn't smell."

After a moment, she got up, and I heard her padding into the kitchen. The faucet turned on. "What kind of tea should we have?" She called to me. I rolled out of bed. "Something soothing," I said as I picked up the two trash bags and dragged them back to the kitchen. Opening the freezer, I stuffed them back in as my mom rifled through the teabags we had left.

"How about sweet rose?"

I nodded. The apartment didn't seem so gray and dim anymore. I fiddled with switches until I figured out how to adjust the brightness of the main light in the living room, so it was warm and bright golden inside. We spent the night playing backgammon while we held our hot mugs of tea. And when we went to sleep, we drew all the blinds until it was completely dark.

Coins

Bailey Stein
From LHSP 125
Nominated by Carol Tell

Bailey's essay is an outstanding example of what "writing to discover" means. He starts with a question he wants to research, and he elegantly and logically constructs an argument around his findings. From his original question ("Is a human coin toss 'random,' or is it, as in a computer coin toss, predetermined?"), he engages in a complex and fascinating discussion about free will. His inquiry into the subject goes above and beyond a typical research essay of this kind.

Carol Tell

Coins

"You are to write a program that simulates a number of coin tosses and then prints the number of heads and the number of tails to the computer's console." Looking back, I was almost certainly half-asleep as I read over the directions to one of my AP Computer Science assignments. With a uniformly rigorous class schedule, my Computer Science class quickly became sort of a refuge from my other less-interesting classes. AP Computer Science wasn't an easy class by any means, but I continuously found intrigue in its seemingly endless supply of gotcha moments. This assignment, like many others, sounded easy enough at first. The most direct approach, I figured, would be to designate half of a numerical range to heads and the other half to tails. I could then just have the computer select a number, within that range, at random. The assignment seemed pretty clear-cut, but what it didn't mention is that computers cannot actually generate random numbers. This was, without a doubt, *the* gotcha moment; instead of being able to just write a few lines of code, I had to do some external research to find the best alternative: using other dynamic numbers as a seed, such as time, to generate pseudo-random numbers. After implementing this alternative, I tested my program by simulating one thousand coin tosses. The results seemed random, but I felt somewhat disappointed knowing that the results were actually deterministic and, on a larger scale, predictable.

Thinking within this perspective leads to a very interesting question: how is a physical coin toss any different than a simulated one? The sheer number of variables affecting a physical toss may seem too overwhelming for reliable predictions, but it would be naive to dismiss the idea that physical coin tosses are just as deterministic as their simulated counterparts. One of the primary themes in *No Country for Old Men* is determinism versus free will, and that's exemplified by Chigurh's two proposed coin tosses during the film. Instead of directly dismissing free will, however, the coin toss in *No Country for Old Men* embodies a greater philosophical question of whether one truly has control over their actions.

Before diving into that philosophical discussion, however, a look into the background of the coin toss seems pertinent. The earliest records of the coin toss trace all the way back to Roman times, when the game was called "navia aut caput," or "ship or head" (Alleyne, 2009). This name is remarkably similar to the widely adopted modern-day name, "heads or tails," likely because both names intuitively reference each side of a coin as an opposite. *The Telegraph* also notes that "A related game, Cross and Pile, was played in medieval England. The cross was the major design on one side of many coins, and the Pile was the mark created by the hammer used to strike the metal on the other side." Clearly the game has been around in an almost entirely static form for quite some time now, so its ubiquity in the modern-day world doesn't come as much of a surprise.

What is surprising, however, is the extent of that ubiquity. In the United States specifically, the coin flip is incredibly common amongst the general public for settling low-stakes disputes. My personal experience in this regard stretches back to the early years of my childhood, when my parents would consistently use coin tosses to settle disputes between my siblings and myself. The disputes were undoubtedly critical for a child—who got to eat the last piece of pie, who had to do an infrequent chore, or who got to go to the baseball game. Of course, these disputes are retroactively frivolous, hence making them low-stake and suitable for "random chance" over a logical approach. Eventually, my siblings and I started believing in a bias towards heads, so my parents largely discontinued the coin toss, as, at that point, it merely served to create another argument. The coin toss continued to play a role at later times throughout my late childhood and adolescence, however. At my high school, for example, I recall one of our teachers offering a ten dollar gift card for whoever could correctly guess the highest number of sequential coin tosses. We played this game at each of our monthly award assemblies, as it was a clever form of entertainment as the administrators prepared their presentations. Since my high school was quite small at around 200 students, this game would only go on for a half dozen to a dozen or so tosses, until everyone but one had guessed incorrectly. This made it feel like a much higher-stake game, when, in reality, each of us were all hoping for the very small chance that we would be the one to guess every toss correctly and receive the ten dollar gift card.

Although the coin flip is most often associated with day-to-day low-stakes disputes, there are numerous times throughout history when crucial decisions were placed merely on how a small piece of metal landed. One of the most notable high-stakes flips occurred during the founding of Portland, Oregon, when its two New England native founders "vied for the bragging rights of naming the 640-acre locale after their respective hometowns" (Rheenen, 2014). In order to decide who received the naming rights to the new city, the founders agreed to a two-out-of-three coin toss, in which the founder wishing to name the city "Portland," of course, won. Another remarkable instance noted by *Mental Floss* is the coin toss between the Wright brothers that decided who would be the first to attempt a flight. Although Wilbur Wright won the coin flip and attempted the first flight on December 14, 1903, he ended up stalling the flyer and diving it into the sand. After the necessary repairs were made, Wilbur's brother, Orville, attempted and succeeded at flying the aircraft, taking the honor of the first successful flight away from his hopeful brother.

More recently, coin tosses have been used in politics, often as a last resort when two candidates receive an equal number of votes. In a city of the Philippines, for example, a mayoral election resulted in two candidates earning 3,236 votes each (Virola, 2013). Following protocol, the election officials flipped a coin five times, and the election went to the candidate who won three of the five flips. It may seem far fetched that coin tosses would ever have an affect on a US election, but that's exactly what happened earlier this year during the Democratic party primaries (Kelly, 2016). In Iowa's Democratic caucus, candidates Hillary Clinton and Bernie Sanders were in a dead heat for the state's delegates, which would ultimately help determine the party's presidential nomination. For every tied precinct, a coin toss was performed in order to declare the winner of that precinct. Amazingly, Hillary Clinton won six out of six coin tosses, helping her expand her lead over Bernie Sanders. While it is generally agreed that these coin tosses did not decide the winner of the Iowa caucus, it's worth noting the surprising significance of the coin toss in this high-stakes scenario. Although arguably not nearly as important as politics, sports is another contentious area where coin tosses are used quite frequently. Most commonly, a coin is tossed at the beginning of the game to decide which team starts, in small events such as middle school soccer games to large events such as the Superbowl. Perhaps the most intriguing toss during a sporting event occurred at a FIFA football match between Colombia and Paraguay. Instead of landing flat on the ground to reveal a decisive result, it landed perfectly on its side (Univision Deportes, 2016) As expected, both the referee and the players were very surprised that the coin didn't bounce to reveal which team would receive starting possession of the ball. This instance in particular represents the almost pure uncertainty that we have when watching a coin toss, even though the actual uncertainty lies in the thrower.

A study conducted by statistician Persi Diaconis confirms this notion; when using a mechanical coin tosser, built for Diaconis by Harvard University engineering students, a coin will always land with the same result (Kestenbaum, 2004). Diaconis asserted that coin flips merely offer pseudo-random results, as their human throwers introduce a few practically unpredictable variables such as height, speed, and angles at which the coin is thrown and caught. In a more recent study from Diaconis, he concludes that the mathematical chances of a coin toss are not actually 50-50, and that it's instead "closer to 51-49, biased toward whatever side was up when the coin was thrown into the air" (Lewis, 2012). This conclusion is not only quite interesting on its own, but it's also proof of concept that coin tosses are only "random" because of humans, which aren't perfectly "random" to begin with.

Just as a computer requires a seed, such as other dynamic numbers, to generate a pseudo-random number, coin tosses require a separate layer of variability to generate pseudo-random results. This distinction may seem trivial at first, but it becomes a wonderfully helpful simplification when taking a closer look at the actual randomness of a coin toss. Diaconis has proven that humans are the seed to the coin toss by showing that mechanical tosses do not vary. Therefore, it is evident that the only sources of variability in a coin toss can be attributed to humans and the medium in which the coin is tossed. To clarify, the latter encompasses how the coin physically behaves after a force is acted upon it. To understand how this might vary, consider how a coin flip would differ in three scenarios: indoors, outdoors on a windy day, and in water. The medium is clearly an important factor, perhaps sometimes just as important as the thrower, but it does not change the actual randomness of a coin toss, despite adding additional variables for consideration. That's because of the widely accepted notion that nature is not random. Although certain aspects of nature like weather may appear random on the surface, it is common knowledge that everything is ultimately just cause-and-effect. While a considerable portion of nature may not be practically predictable with currently available tools and technology, it would most certainly still be predictable on a larger scale. Science has long and consistently backed this idea of natural determinism, so it is safe to assume that much of the general public understands nature as having no conscious. Where the contention begins, however, is when we consider whether the variables introduced by humans are deterministic. Those variables are deterministic if and only if humans do not have free will. However, if our thoughts and sequential actions are in fact deterministic, the coin toss cannot possibly be random by any measure.

These assertions may sound overly audacious, so it is important to take a step back and consider supporting logical evidence. If free will does exist, it would be impossible to predict the thoughts of an inherently non-deterministic conscious. Although the variables introduced by nature would be deterministic, as discussed earlier, the coin tosser with free will would have the highest level of control, thereby presenting themselves as a perfectly random seed. The manner in which they throw the coin would be totally unpredictable, as they would freely think of and proceed with their toss without any binding external influence. This would mean that, even if they were taught to throw a coin in a very particular way, they could always just freely change their mind before throwing. Since free will absolutely cannot be predictable, this would suggest that coin tosses are, after all, actually random since their seeds would include fickle free will humans.

The alternative argument that humans do not have free will is admittedly much more nihilistic as it presents some tough moral questions. Within scope, however, if humans are deterministic, meaning that our thoughts and actions are merely an unchangeable result of the cumulation of external stimuli, the coin toss is, by extension, deterministic. This would indicate that someone's thoughts and actions are predictable; it is important to emphasis, however, that it is not currently practical to do so. With that said, being impractical by current technology standards does not equate to being impossible. By definition, determinism would still be predictable, despite requiring a larger scale. Therefore, the variables in which a human presents in a coin toss would also be absolutely predictable. Both the amount and breadth of those variables would certainly be overwhelming, but, again, their yes-or-no ability to be predicted would remain unchanged. Therefore, a deterministic human seed would be of definite pseudo-randomness, as the only "randomness" involved would merely be a result of a kind of deterministic chaos. That is to say, the results would seem random, but would not actually be random, much like how a computer behaves.

Some people very passionately support either free will or determinism, while some others claim there is a middle ground between the two. In a survey conducted by *Scientific American*, 58.9% of respondents said that "we have free will," while the remaining 41.1% said that "we do not have free will." A compilation of respondent comments reveals the primary arguments for each side. While free will is difficult to support with evidence, the main argument claims that we essentially have free will...because we do. Some believe that we are in total control over our conscious thoughts and actions, because it quite frankly feels like we are. This is an understandable argument for free will, but determinism offers a somewhat stronger argument by applying everything we know about everything else in nature to humans. The main argument for determinism states that we are merely highly sophisticated zombies that feel as if we have control. The entire premise of this argument is that the influence of external stimuli will only affect an individual's brain in a single way and that that individual cannot freely change how they think and what they do. Unlike free will, there is a small amount of scientific evidence for determinism; a fairly recent study conducted by a number of neuroscientists at the Institute for Human Cognitive and Brain Sciences in Leipzig, Germany revealed that brain activity can be analyzed to "predict decisions before they are consciously made" (Smith, 2008). One of the lead researchers commented that if decisions are being made up to ten seconds in advance as the data shows, then "there's not much space for free will to operate."

The relationship between the free will vs determinism debate and the coin toss, especially as it is presented in *No Country for Old Men*, is remarkable. In *No Country for Old Men* specifically, free will vs determinism is one of the primary themes and, although the idea of free will is not directly dismissed in the film, it is most definitely called into question. The film suggests that Anton doesn't feel responsible for his murders, that Llewelyn can't prevent himself from returning to the crime scene and running away in the manner in which he does, and that Sheriff Bell can't help but feel apathetic because of everything he has been exposed to throughout his career. At the same time, the film hints at some amount of free will; in one of the very final scenes, for example, Carla Jean rejects an alternative fate offered to her by Anton via a coin toss. While it's difficult to objectively determine what exactly the film is suggesting, my perception of the film is that it's leaning towards determinism while simultaneously asking the audience to draw their own conclusions.

The iconic coin toss at the Texaco gas station is an almost perfect embodiment of the greater philosophical question of whether one truly has control over their actions. The scene is beautifully constructed, has a somewhat awkward feel, and, most importantly, demonstrates how we place so much on such a small object, expecting a random result, when, in reality, it is very possible that the outcome is pseudo-random and entirely destined. Anton appears to recognize some level of determinism; he exits the scene by stating that the older gentleman shouldn't place the coin in his pocket, since it's his lucky coin and that if he does, it will just become another coin, which he later concludes with "which it is." This dialogue suggests that Anton is aware of the irony in placing such a major decision in the hands of what appears to be just a bunch of deterministic chaos.

Not every question has an answer and the question of whether a coin toss is actually random is no exception. What many consider to be a trivial way to solve a dispute is actually an encompassment of a much larger philosophical discussion, one that requires you to consider if we are any different from a pseudo-random seed used by computers. Regardless of where you stand on the amount of free will humans have, it's difficult to avoid questioning why we toss small pieces of metal to remove ourselves from the decision-making process, only to leave it in the hands of a perceived level of "randomness."

Works Cited

Alleyne, Richard. "Coin tossing through the ages." *The Telegraph*, Telegraph Media Group, Dec. 2009, www.telegraph.co.uk/news/science/science-news/6911921/Coin-tossing-through-the-ages.html.

Kelly, Jon. "When the flip of a coin wins an election." *BBC News,* Feb. 2016, www.bbc.com/news/magazine-35473068.

Kestenbaum, David. "The Not So Random Coin Toss." *NPR*, Feb. 2004, www.npr.org/templates/story/story.php?storyId=1697475.

Lewis, Dan. "Gamblers Take Note: The Odds in a Coin Flip Aren't Quite 50/50." *Smithsonian.com*, Smithsonian Institution, Nov. 2012, www.smithsonianmag.com/science-nature/gamblers-take-note-the-odds-in-a-coin-flip-arent-quite-5050-145465423/.

No Country for Old Men. Dir. Ethan Coen and Josh Coen. Perf. Tommy Lee Jones, Javier Bardem, Josh Brolin. Paramount, 2007. Digital Stream.

Rheenen, Erik van. "4 Coin Flips That Changed History." *Mental Floss*, Jun. 2014, mentalfloss.com/article/50832/4-coin-flips-changed-history.

Smith, Kerri. "Brain makes decisions before you even know it." *Nature.com*, Macmillan Publishers, Apr. 2008, www.nature.com/news/2008/080411/full/news.2008.751.html.

Stix, Gary. "Site Survey Shows 60 Percent Think Free Will Exists. Read Why." *Scientific American Blog Network*, Jan. 2015, blogs.scientificamerican.com/talking-back/site-survey-shows-60-percent-think-free-will-exists-read-why/.

Univision Deportes. "Insólito: la moneda cayó parada en el sorteo del partido Colombia vs Paraguay." YouTube, July 2016, www.youtube.com/watch?v=HH7tTR2Nv5E.

Virola, Madonna. "Coin toss breaks tie in mayoral race in Oriental Mindoro town." *INQUIRER*, May 2013, newsinfo.inquirer.net/410339/coin-toss-breaks-tie-in-mayoral-race-in-oriental-mindoro-town.

Granader Family Prize for Excellence in Multilingual Writing

The Molecular Connection between Chemistry and Learning Astronomy

Xiaowei Ou
From Writing 120
Nominated by Shuwen Li

In his first semester during the freshman year, Xiaowei got interested in astronomy and was surprised that his professor asked him to study chemistry in order to become an astronomist. With such a curiosity and ambition in astronomy, Xiaowei conducted in-depth research on the connection between chemistry and learning astronomy. This essay is shaped into a traditional academic paper; on the other hand, the essay adopts a light tone and communicates disciplinary knowledge in plain language that is accessible to a lay audience. Step by step, Xiaowei unpacks the interrelationship between chemistry and astronomy through synthesizing numerous scholarly articles. One feature of this essay is the dialogues that Xiaowei wove into it. Those dialogues become a bridge connecting Xiaowei and his audience. Upon finishing reading this essay, you might be motivated to become an amateur astronomist as Xiaowei aspires.

Shuwen Li

The Molecular Connection between Chemistry and Learning Astronomy

Have you ever wondered what is out there in the universe when you look up in the sky at night? Have you ever considered studying astronomy because you only want to enjoy looking at the Milky Way? However, is it true that astronomists only do stargazing to explore the universe? The answer is, no doubt, no. Rather than just doing stargazing, astronomy is much more complicated and interrelated to other subjects, including physics, chemistry, mathematics, and even biology. Among all these fields of study, each of them has its specific playground in astronomy.

I came to the realization of this fact only after I started shadowing an astronomy department professor in a study dedicated to identifying astronomical structures in our Galaxy. It amazed me so much when I was told that we were not going to use any telescope or do any stargazing for this entire research. Even more unexpected, the first literature I was assigned to was a chemistry textbook. Perplexed, I thought about directly expressing my doubt to the professor, but I hesitated. Somehow, I knew I would not get what I want by simply asking for it. Instead, I turned to the many resources in libraries and decided to convince myself with my own research.

Now, with all my confusion resolved, I want to share what I discovered and shed some light on the chemistry involved in astronomy research. Please follow my steps to uncover this spectacular world of the treasure of astronomy and chemistry. For your best experience, this journey shall start with the most shining gem—the key concept that binds everything together.

Setting off my research by first looking for a key concept that will link chemistry and astronomy, I got exactly what I wanted – molecules. From here, I gradually formed my first answer to my initial question. The most primary discipline of chemistry is studying and understanding molecules, while in astronomy, the exploration of the universe is, to a great extent, the exploration of the molecules in the universe. Now, you may wonder how is this answer going to fit into the big puzzle between astronomy and chemistry. Let me introduce the concept of interstellar clouds, widely and thoroughly studied parts of the universe. Interstellar clouds exist everywhere. People tend to believe there is nothing among stars, while in reality such presumed empty space is filled with molecules, though usually in a lower density (Fraser, McCoustra, & Williams, 2002, p. 2.11). I acknowledge that this statement may be unbelievable to you for the first sight, but an obvious example could prove my statement in a few seconds. As I sometimes look into the sky at night, some stars would suddenly disappear even without clouds and reappear after a few days. Here, interstellar clouds are the naughty kids who block the light from a distant star and prevent us from seeing it.

In most cases, these clouds themselves are invisible to naked human eyes, but astronomists have specific instruments to capture the existence of these clouds. You can imagine that these clouds can talk to you. They transmit information that astronomers are desperate to learn. For a particular study in Orion, astronomists "map the emission from a number of complex organic molecules, to estimate the molecular abundances, and to address some important aspects of the molecular complexity in Orion" (Baudry, Brouillet, & Despois, 2016, p. 976). In making this comment, this particular research acknowledges the extensive information about Orion that we can get by observing the molecules from it. I found this interesting and informative because the result may be compared to what we already knew about our solar system. Astronomists suggest a great possibility in establishing some links between the organic molecules and early terrestrial life (Öberg, 2016, p. 9632).

"Why interstellar clouds?", some astronomy beginners may question, "Can't we study something else to explore the universe?" The answer is that interstellar clouds are related to all astronomical phenomenon in the sky. The molecules that composed the clouds will eventually, if not once, become part of a star, a planet, or a galaxy. This life cycle of space matter shows me how studies of all kinds of astronomical objects resemble the study of interstellar clouds, including theoretical models, laboratory experiments and observational data obtained in these aspects of astronomical research. From there, I believe such characteristics of interstellar clouds can prove its vitality in astronomy.

While it is true that studies in the quantum mechanics and particle behaviors do not necessarily involve interstellar clouds anymore, those studies are far too advanced and complicated for an astronomy beginner. Therefore, I decided to put it aside because it should not be the primary concern of astronomy beginners reading this article. If this makes sense to you, the importance of chemistry in learning astronomy should be a little bit clear now, but do not be in a hurry. I will have detail explanation on several actual research areas in astronomy to illustrate my point better here.

Going back to the study of the very beginning of the universe, the study of the universe is essentially the study of molecules. As the universe evolves, the molecules that flow in it also evolve. Astronomists can trace the transition of all the molecules in the universe to get a better understanding of the transition of the universe itself. I discovered that the places they are most interested in are the interstellar clouds. Numerous research has been conducted on the related topics, and most of them follow chemical molecules as a lead to the result, including research of complex organic interstellar molecules (Herbst & van Dishoeck, 2009, p. 428). To make this clearer, the complexity of the molecules in the universe, in fact grows as the universe ages. The most direct evidence would be the number of atoms in a single molecule, which increases as they exist for a longer time. Putting it in another way, our universe now processes molecules with great complexity, reaching almost 400 species, among which include molecules containing up to 12 atoms. Still, we cannot deny the possibility of more undiscovered species of molecules (Fraser et al., 2002, p. 2.12). Even more, as the universe continues aging, the process of forming complex molecules in deep space will also carry on. Then I dug deeper into scholarly journals to see how all this understanding and knowledge about space molecules is applied in the actual scientific studies. I was surprised by the wide application of space molecules and the connection between chemistry and astronomy.

On a large scale, the early Galaxy represents an excellent example of such a research approach. The related research follows the same rule of finding the chemical signature at the beginning of Galaxy by looking at the interstellar clouds, which composed mostly of different types of molecules. More accurately, one study compares the chemistries of stars in the Milky Way dwarf spheroidal satellite galaxies with stars in the Galaxy (Venn et al., 2004, p. 1189). The study claims that stars in the dwarf galaxies are distinctively different from those in the Galaxy, which may suggest some different forming processes. For me, this means something more than that. I would rather argue that the differences present a new way of understanding chemical reactions in different environments, which are crucial for the development of chemistry.

On a minor level, the atoms in the molecules are also powerful evidence for stellar development and transformation. The universe started with only helium, and all the other heavier elements were created gradually as generations and generations of stars formed and died, including our Sun. One study focuses on the chemical abundances of one specific star, the Sun (Lodders, 2003, p. 1245). The researcher believes this will help us better understand the evolution of the Sun, a belief that will assist us in learning about chemical process under extreme conditions—in this case, inside a burning star.

In fact, similar studies have proven a reciprocal relationship between astronomy and chemistry. The results we get from the similar research will eventually give astronomists a better understanding about the nucleosynthesis of the elements in different stars in dwarf galaxies, Galaxy—and through the universe. In both cases I mentioned above, knowledge of astronomy helps astronomists understand the chemical formation about astronomical objects that are accessible to us. Later, a synthesized knowledge of chemistry and astronomy will facilitate understanding other subjects that are too far away from us for detailed observation and measurement.

Next, I want to talk about the main character of the universe—stars.

Just like houses they are built up from bricks. Ultimately, all the stars are formed out of interstellar clouds. As the density of the interstellar clouds gets to a certain level, a new star might form. Astronomists are interested in studying such high-density areas, which they call star-forming region. It turns out that the molecules play a significant role in helping the star formation not only because they are the raw material but also because many of the chemical properties they own could trigger and accelerate the whole star formation process. Nevertheless, I wonder more about what these little assistants in star formation could reveal between chemistry and astronomy.

Depending on different scales, astronomists are interested in various ranges of star-forming regions. From one of the smallest—our earth and solar system—to the huge spiral arm of M51, astronomists discuss various chemical molecules that show distinctive characteristics in forming stars. Orion nebula, for example, was studied in CO and $CO/H2$ ratio (Baudry et al., 2016, p. 980). The solar system and Earth are considered in mostly the organic elements such as C, H, N (Ehrenfreund & Charnley, 2000, p. 428). The spiral arm of M51 addresses the problem regarding the discontinuity between the star formation rate and two distinct molecular species, CH_3OH and HNCO (Watanabe, Sakai, Sorai, Ueda, & Yamamoto, 2016, p. 145).

In these different studies, if we look close enough, we will see how different scales of research on star-forming region involve varying degrees of chemistry. I would describe these as different fruits dangling on the same tree. Though generally studying the molecules that are acting in the process of star formation, astronomy focuses on various scales of chemical molecules properties presentation in a different environment, which usually involves different kinds of methods and modeling.

Despite the scale size of those studies, one thing that does not change are molecules, which are always the main subjects in the study of star forming region. We use the best language we have, chemistry, to decrypt them and find out what they are capable of in helping star formation.

As I pushed forward and dug deeper into the research on astronomy, I uncovered a new concept called "protoplanetary disk," which is quite similar to the star-forming region but poses a different indication on the connection between chemistry and astronomy. Although called star-forming region, it is an area where a star has a chance to form. For those places where stars are already forming, things are different. Protoplanetary disks are places where molecules are even denser and have already started to form a star or planet. Astronomists study these protoplanetary disks in pursuit of the distinctive reactions of the molecules in the disks. As the star formation has already begun, the most important thing is no longer the property of the molecules themselves but how they behave differently in the violent environment of protoplanetary disks. As I proposed earlier, since astronomists want to learn the detailed information inside the disk, molecules are excellent sources.

Astronomists choose different molecules for studying different protoplanetary disks based on which molecule will help reflect the situation more accurately. In some cases, for examples, they examined the CO isotopologues in interstellar clouds and circumstellar disks (Visser, Dishoeck, & Black, 2009, p. 342). In other cases, they may study lead isotope for a young formation age of the Earth-Moon system (Connelly & Bizzarro, 2016, p. 40).

Not only can molecules tell us the information regarding now existing protoplanetary disks, but it can also give us an idea of protoplanetary disk that existed in the past. More specifically, our Earth-Moon system nowadays still process evidence for astronomists to discover the history of it (Connelly & Bizzarro, 2016, p. 40). In other words, molecules can help find out when the earth and moon developed into their current form. Astronomists explore the timing of the giant impact by seeking for the loss of volatile Pb relative to refractory U. With some careful configurations in simulation, astronomists can determine the more accurate age of the moon and what happened right after the huge impact and before the moon finally formed and got stabilized. I was excited when I found out how a single ratio of elements could tell us things that happened before human beings even started to exist. Isn't this amazing? I wonder if it's possible to rebuild the formation process, in the past, in our Galaxy, and even in the entire universe, with some simple but precise measurement on some other similar chemical properties throughout the space.

Now, I hope we agree that chemistry plays a significant role in studying astronomy. As far as I could tell, after going through all my research, the study of molecules constitutes a great part of the fundamental topics in astronomy. Among these topics, each of them presents me a distinct connection between chemistry and astronomy. Although I only went through three of them, they have already shocked me and led me to this complex and strong net between chemistry and astronomy.

As the most fundamental part of space molecules research, interstellar clouds pervade every study area astronomists get to, just as they pervade the seemingly empty universe. With a thorough understanding of molecules in interstellar clouds, astronomists then move on to areas regarding early universe formation, in which astronomy and chemistry improve each other. In the study of the star-forming region, we learn that chemistry has different levels of involvement in astronomy, depending on the scale of study. In the study of protoplanetary disks, astronomists examine the region where stars or planets are already forming. I discovered the fact that chemistry not only informs the present but also indicates the past of an astronomical subject if we acquire enough information.

Granted, these topics are not the single fields studied in astronomy. I maintain that they are the most relevant topics to beginners. These topics are what astronomy beginners will inevitably face and go through at the very beginning of their astronomy study (Fraser, McCoustra, & Williams, 2002, p. 2.11). The utilization of chemistry and study of chemical molecules in astronomy is only partially covered in my above argument. However, I see that more areas of chemistry will be synthesized into astronomy in the future. I hope more students who are interested in studying astronomy can join the study of chemistry in order to enjoy the spectacular journey of discovering the universe. Having acknowledged such connections, students will be better prepared for whatever comes forward along their journey. Now, I will go back to my chemistry textbook.

Reference

Acke, B., & E. van den Ancker, M. (2004). ISO spectroscopy of disks around Herbig Ae/Be stars. *Astronomy & Astrophysics, 426*(1), 151–170. doi:10.1051/0004-6361:20040400

Baudry, A., Brouillet, N., & Despois, D. (2016). Star formation and chemical complexity in the Orion nebula: A new view with the IRAM and ALMA interferometers. *Comptes Rendus Physique, 17*(9), 976–984. doi:10.1016/j.crhy.2016.07.019

Connelly, J. N., & Bizzarro, M. (2016). Lead isotope evidence for a young formation age of the Earth–Moon system. *Earth and Planetary Science Letters, 452*, 36–43. doi:10.1016/j.epsl.2016.07.010

Dutrey, A., Guilloteau, S., & Guelin, M. (1997). Chemistry of protosolar-like nebulae: The molecular content of the DM Tau and GG Tau disks. *Astronomy and Astrophysics, 317*, L55-L58.

Ehrenfreund, P., & Charnley, S. B. (2000). Organic molecules in the interstellar medium, comets, and meteorites: A voyage from dark clouds to the early earth. *Annual Review of Astronomy and Astrophysics, 38*(1), 427–483.

Fraser, H. J., McCoustra, M. R. S., & Williams, D. A. (2002). The molecular universe. *Astronomy & Geophysics, 43*(2), 2.10-2.18. doi:10.1046/j.1468-4004.2002.43210.x

Garrod, R. T., Weaver, S. L. W., & Herbst, E. (2008). Complex chemistry in star-forming regions: An expanded gas-grain warm-up chemical model. *The Astrophysical Journal, 682*(1), 283-302. doi:10.1086/588035

Gómez-Ruiz, A. I., Codella, C., Viti, S., Jiménez-Serra, I., Navarra, G.,
Bachiller, R., ... Nisini, B. (2016). Diagnosing shock temperature with
NH3 and H2O profiles. *Monthly Notices of the Royal Astronomical
Society, 462*(2), 2203–2217. doi:10.1093/mnras/stw1811

Herbst, E., & van Dishoeck, E. F. (2009). Complex organic interstellar
molecules. *Annual Review of Astronomy and Astrophysics, 47*(1),
427–480. doi:10.1146/annurev-astro-082708-101654

Lodders, K. (2003). Solar system abundances and condensation temperatures of
the elements. *The Astrophysical Journal, 591*(2), 1220-1247.
doi:10.1086/375492

Öberg, K. I. (2016). Photochemistry and astrochemistry: Photochemical
pathways to interstellar complex organic molecules. *Chemical Reviews,
116*(17), 9631–9663. doi:10.1021/acs.chemrev.5b00694

Richings, A. J., & Schaye, J. (2016). Chemical evolution of giant molecular
clouds in simulations of galaxies. *Monthly Notices of the Royal
Astronomical Society, 460*(3), 2297–2321. doi:10.1093/mnras/stw1135

Venn, K. A., Irwin, M., Shetrone, M. D., Tout, C. A., Hill, V., & Tolstoy,
E. (2004). Stellar chemical signatures and hierarchical galaxy formation.
The Astronomical Journal, 128(3), 1177-1195. doi:10.1086/422734

Visser, R., Dishoeck, E. F. van, & Black, J. H. (2009). The photodissociation
and chemistry of CO isotopologues: applications to interstellar clouds
and circumstellar disks. *Astronomy & Astrophysics, 503*(2), 323–343.
doi:10.1051/0004-6361/200912129

Watanabe, Y., Sakai, N., Sorai, K., Ueda, J., & Yamamoto, S. (2016). Molecular
distribution in the spiral arm of M51. *The Astrophysical Journal,
819*(2), 144-154. doi:10.3847/0004-637X/819/2/144

It Is More Than Just Ketchup: Comparative Analysis of Two Print Advertisements

Fengyi Tong

From Writing 120

Nominated by Scott Beal

Fengyi Tong's essay tackles a subject that is challenging for its apparent triviality; ketchup is not the kind of product one might expect to reveal large cultural differences in its advertising. But through her attention to detail and her thoughtful consideration of not only WHAT the two ads ask us to think, but HOW they ask us to think, Tong makes her case compelling and persuasive.

Scott Beal

It Is More Than Just Ketchup:
Comparative Analysis of Two Print Advertisements

Ketchup is made in a way that might be much more standard than your expectation: no matter where it is made, no matter which brand it belongs to, there is no fundamental difference between them. From production process to taste, ketchup is duplicated all over the world. Since the products promoted are identical, our comparison of two ketchup ads, one from America, one from China, could focus on the strategic and cultural difference, instead of the differences of products themselves.

The American ad is produced by Heinz Company, which, according to Forbes, is "the market leader, with an 82% market share in the UK and a 60% share in the US market". The ad of this famous company is impressively innovative. Against the red background, stands a classical Heinz ketchup bottle. Unlike ordinary one, this ketchup bottle is horizontally sliced into a stack of fresh tomatoes pieces. These slices are not placed in order. Rather, they are slightly messy, enabling audience to the edges of

some pieces which suggest the juicy and fresh interior of the tomatoes. The top of the bottle is made of a tomato slice with leaves, making it more credible that the bottle is made of natural tomatoes instead of glasses. If we zoom in a little bit, we can tell the leaves are fairly green and strong, which leave the impression that the tomato has just been picked up from the farm.

On the surface of this ketchup bottle, the classical logo of Heinz is stamped in the front, showing the brand as well as food name in big, capital letters. These labels are the very same with those stamped on every Heinz ketchup that we could see almost everyday. Consumers are so familiar with this outer packing that they can recognize which brand this commercial is promoting for at the first glance. In this way, this ad is effective in impressing the audience with the image of their brand.

The ketchup bottle is located on a vivid red background, with white text "No one grows ketchup like Heinz." on the bottom. This phrase perfectly corresponds to the picture by innovatively using the word "grow" instead of "produce". As we all know, that ketchup is produced in the factory, not harvested from a farm. By using this rhetoric, this ad sets up the illusion that ketchup is not artificial product, but natural, healthy agricultural product, just like fresh tomatoes that are actually "grown". Moreover, the expression "No one … like Heinz" not only states that Heinz has special focus on health but also implies that it is the best in this field. Buying this product is the smartest choice you could make if you are concerned about healthier lifestyle. Along with the sliced ketchup bottle, this ad aims to change consumer's traditional impression on their ketchup, transforming it from sugary flavoring loaded with preservative to fresh, wholesome food.

In comparison, the Chinese advertisement conveys more pieces of information besides health. The right half of this printing is a little boy sitting in front of a table, using the ketchup to draw the pattern of a cute crab on omelet rice. Holding the plastic squeeze bottle upside down, the little boy is squeezing out the ketchup quiet effortlessly, which could tell from the fluent lines of the pattern he makes. Additionally,

he only uses one hand to squeeze it while he dips his fingers of another hand in the tomato sauce to have a taste of the ketchup. The picture that even a little boy can easily squeeze out the ketchup with only one hand, instead of two, implies the convenience the new squeeze bottle package could bring to consumers. The ad also suggests that with the new design, people can have fun with their product without the difficulty of getting the ketchup out from traditional glass bottles. With his smile and eyes looking down, the boy in the printing looks delighted and interested, revealing that he is immersing himself in the fun of decorating the omelet rice with ketchup. These details together illustrate that consumers can not only facilitate the use of ketchup, but also bring fun to you and your family.

On the left part, there are sentences in red reading "with just one squeeze, here you get the delicacy "(挤一挤，就美味) and "Ah Omelet rice, is the thing that enables me to squeeze a lot, lot of McCormick ketchup to eat!" (蛋包饭啊，就是可以让我挤好多好多的味好美番茄酱来吃!) Written in a special print like ketchup with attractive gloss, the first sentence highlights the characteristic and convenience of the new design as well as the good taste of the product. The second sentence is written in a very cute and lively font, with characters tilting to different directions and words printed in various sizes. The tone of this sentence is informal and verbal, trying to imitate the expression style of children. These arrangements lead the audience to believe that this sentence is spoken by the boy in the picture, adding voice to this silent, printing ad.

In addition, the Chinese ad shows the audience a way to use ketchup: you could use it to make omelet rice, responding to the special need of Chinese market. Ketchup, although it has almost become part of American tradition, is not used that frequently in Chinese daily dishes. Chinese people, generally speaking, mainly consume ketchup in McDonald's or some other restaurants instead of using them in home cooking. By introducing a way to do home cooking with ketchup, the ad aims to popularize the product among Chinese families, a big potential market that has not been well exploited yet. Choosing a little boy having fun with ketchup in a house-like environment also serves for this target audience. Parents might be attracted because of their admiration of the happy family life shown in the ad, while children audience might also want to have fun with ketchup just like the boy in the ad does. The background is very obscure so that it is hard to see behind the boy. However, the white color of the backdrop leaves the audience the impression of cleanness, setting up the image that the product is high-class. At the down right corner are three signs on the ketchup package: one is the "green food" mark, another one is for HACCP food safety control system certification, and the last one is the sign of "Famous brand" identified by government. Next to these signs, the description "healthy, without additives" is printed in a small size.

Although targeting consumers of different countries, these two ads still have something in common. For example, both of them try to make the ketchup in the picture looks delicious and alluring. And they also employed very similar methods for this effect, including lighting, usage of color, etc. In addition, these two respond to the audience's concern of health by stating that their products are free of additive. Nevertheless, the way to create this image is quiet different.

The way employed by the American ad is very conceptual and innovative. In the ad, this famous brand tries to change its long-established image as a common condiment into healthy gourmet by a tomato-slice ketchup bottle and a concise annotation. If people think about it carefully, they will find it lacks supporting evidence and promise. Do they actually decrease the amount of sugar and preservative used in the factory? No one knows since the ad does not reply to that question directly. Rather, the ad just focuses on making the impression that its product is healthy on the targeted audience, which could be very vague but can influence the consumers in the long term. As far as I am concerned, this strategy is effective to convey this idea. Instead of claiming the ketchup is healthy directly, which undoubtedly is skeptical, the ad gives these suggestive clues. They together lead audience to associate Heinz ketchup with health quality unconsciously. Moreover, the ad sets up the illusion that consumers themselves come to the conclusion "Heinz ketchup is healthy" with their own observation and thinking, not persuaded by the company. When they think of Heinz ketchup in the future, this stack of sliced tomato might replace the ingredient on fries or a burger in their head, whose credibility will be seldom questioned since it is their "own opinion".

In comparison, the Chinese ad offers more solid evidence towards its claim. Instead of creating some image, the ad simply put some certification signs, demonstrating that the product's healthy quality has been proved by some authoritative institutions. In this way, the ad reassures the consumers by dissolving their doubt of the authenticity of the claim. This method is frequently used in Chinese ads, no matter if it is a commercial or printing ad. Companies are very active in applying for the qualifications issued by authoritative institutions, not to mention showing them to consumers afterwards. Compared to America, China is a more conservative society which emphasizes more on authority and prevention of uncertainty. So when faced with consumers' suspicion of products' quality or effect, slogans like "expert tested" or "certificated" are very effective to win Chinese consumers' trust because that is exactly what they give credibility to.

On the other hand, American society emphasizes less on authority's voice but more on individual thinking. Thus, American consumers tend to be more open to new ideas and have low uncertainty avoidance. As result, Heinz, as a company that has long been perceived as a producer of unhealthy sugary condiments, can try to set up a brand new image in front of consumers just with a conceptual ad. No specific fact, statistics or any recognition from authoritative institutions are included. Just a sliced ketchup bottle and a slogan are presented, which is apparently far from enough to persuade suspicious Chinese audiences, but seems enough to impress American audiences by its innovative slogan and picture. Novelty and leading of individual thinking, instead of bored presentation of authoritative opinion, might be more successful in raising American consumers' interest.

While "healthy" is only one attribute pointed out in the American ad, the Chinese ad covers more than that: health, brand reputation, taste, and way to cook. It even implies that the ketchup can bring fun to children and families. Why is the amount of information loaded so different? This can be explained by the different thinking ways of eastern and western people. According to Beichen Liang, who studies philosophy in business administration, several tests on ad information processing show that "Eastern Asians tend to think holistically and Western people tend to think analytically". In other words, Eastern Asians are more likely to identify relationships among elements in ads and will recall more information than Western people. Even though exposed to several different attributes, westerners generally only focus on one or two of them and the rest of the information will be ignored. As result, the best way to promote is limiting the amount of information in the ad. Presenting one or two pieces of information that company wants to convey most into the ad in an impressive way might be the optimal choice for US advertising agencies. But for Chinese audiences, they could absorb more information at once. So a holistic ad will be more effective in China market because a larger group can be attracted by more attributes shown. That might explain why the Chinese ad conveys much more information in just one poster.

Although ketchup is identical everywhere, the ketchup ads vary from country to country, according to the different cultural backgrounds of local audience. When different weight is given to authority and individual thinking, when people have different styles of information processing, successful ads can never be produced on an assembly line like ketchup. Not only advertising agencies, but also everyone including us, should adjust ways of expression to the traits of targeted audiences.

Works cited

"Heinz $28 Bn Acquisition Implies Faster Global Growth And Thicker Margins Ahead", *Forbes*, www.forbes.com/sites/greatspeculations/2013/02/15/ heinz-28-bn-acquisition-implies-faster-global-growth-and-thicker-mar gins-ahead/#2ca26c922a16, Accessed 20 Nov. 2016.

Liang, Beichen, "Cultural differences in ad information processing: The influence of analytic versus holistic thinking". Dissertations, University of Illinois at Chicago, 2007

Xiao Qingyun, "A Comparative Study of Cultural Values of Chinese and U. S. Advertisements", *Journal of Huizhou University*, Vol.25, No.14, 2005, pp. 94-98

"Semiotic Analysis of Advertising", adv91peternguyenpham.wordpress.com/2014/09/22/semiotic-analysis-of-advertising/, Accessed 20 Nov. 2016.

The American ad is from www.frederiksamuel.com/blog/2007/12/heinz-ketchup.html

The Chinese ad is from www.weihaomei.com/index.jsp

Granader Family Prize for Outstanding Writing Portfolio

Stephanie Bloom - Writing100

stephaniebloomwriting1002016.wordpress.com

Stephanie Bloom
From Writing 100
Nominated by Gina Brandolino

It is my pleasure to nominate Stephanie Bloom's exceptional e-portfolio for the Granader Family Portfolio Prize. Steph and another student tied for first place in the class vote for e-portfolio in a class that produced a number of truly competitive e-portfolios. Steph is a student in the Stamps School of Art and Design, and her talent for visual projects is plainly evident in her e-portfolio. But her e-portfolio isn't just visually appealing—its content shows the work of a writer pushing herself, not taking the easy way out, choosing topics that mean something to her and engaging with them deeply. The result is that her e-portfolio is equally delightful to look at—to experience visually—and also to read. Here is what some of her classmates had to say why they voted for her e-portfolio: Her welcome page is very detailed and personal, featuring many of her own pictures. Her prefaces are thorough, and her writing has an honesty that makes it engaging. Her knowledge of art and graphics is clear. There's so much other stuff to explore besides the assignments! It is obvious that Steph dedicated a lot of her time to her e-portfolio. As much as I enjoyed—and more, admired—all of Steph's papers, I am most enthusiastic about her work for the fifth assignment. This assignment, the last one in the class, asked students to identify a group of writers they felt they could offer writing advice to and compose a list of tips addressed to them. Steph's "Advice to Writers Who Are in Creative Majors" is simply amazing. Don't take my word for it; go have a look.

Gina Brandolino

Stephanie Bloom - Writing 100
Scroll down for more exciting stuff

Search On This Site

Search ...

HAPPY HOLIDAYS

Link to 100 of the greatest christmas songs ever! -

Blog Stats

281 Hits

Hey there!

September 29, 2016
Leave a comment

Hello and welcome to my e-portfolio! Here you will find my assignments for Writing 100, and other bits and bobs too. Feel free to look around, click on any tabs, and leave me comments – I love feedback!

A Bit About Me:

My name's Stephanie Bloom and I'm a current freshman at the University of Michigan. I've lived my whole life in London until now, so please bear with my perhaps "alternative" spellings – e.g., we spell color like... colour. My dad grew up in the suburbs of New York, which is what triggered me to explore this other part of me and come to college in America. That technically makes me half New Yorker and half Londoner, despite never having

Advice to Writers Who Are in Creative Majors

The "creative types" tend to be slightly more right-brained → as this is the creative hemisphere.

However, sometimes this can mean that language and writing (which is located in the left hemisphere) doesn't come as naturally to us.

However, this is not always the case! It is just a trend and even then it's still important to understand that us creatives can offer a lot to writing.

Tip Number 1: Use your creativity in your words- this is what comes more naturally to us so do not HIDE IT! Even if it's a research paper.

Tip Number 2: Don't stress out over punctuation, spelling and grammar nearly as much as you do! The most important aspect of your work is your ideas and originally.

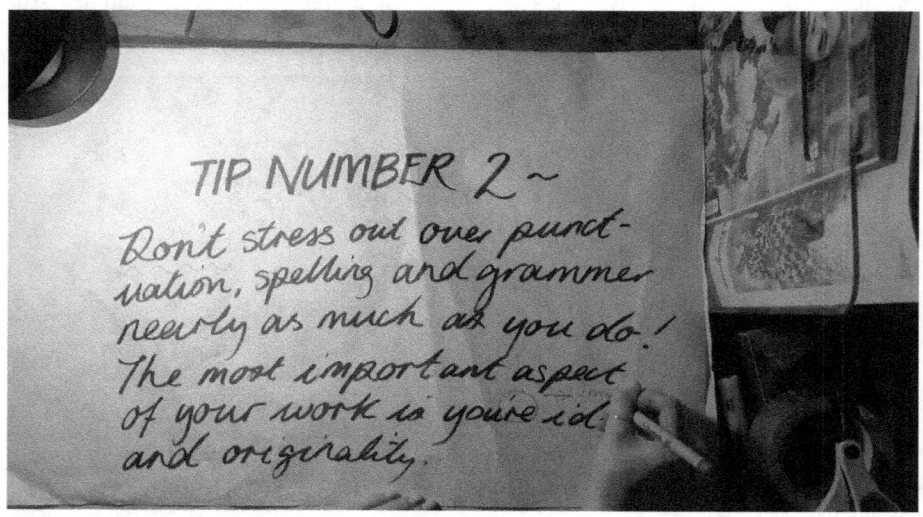

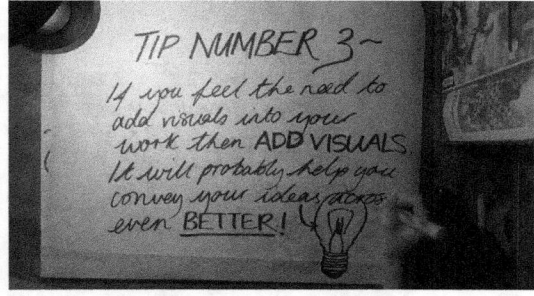

Tip Number 3: If you feel the need to add visuals into your work then ADD VISUALS. It will probably help you convey your ideas across even BETTER!

Tip Number 4: OK- but this doesn't mean spending ages choosing a font- even if you're a perfectionist.

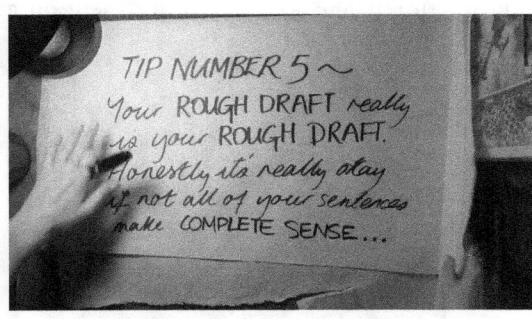

Tip Number 5: Your ROUGH DRAFT really is your ROUGH DRAFT. Honestly it's really okay if not all of your sentences make COMPLETE SENSE…

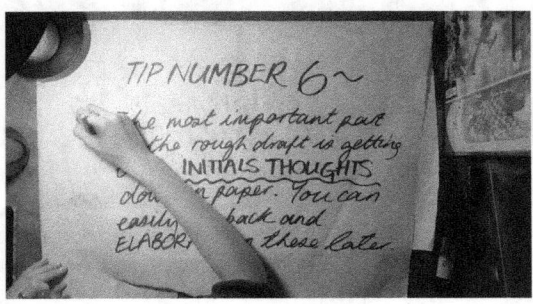

Tip Number 6: The most important part of the rough draft is getting those INITIAL THOUGHTS down on paper. You can easily go back and elaborate on these later.

Your rough draft is only the skeleton of your final piece. Use it to explore your ideas not to perfect your ideas.

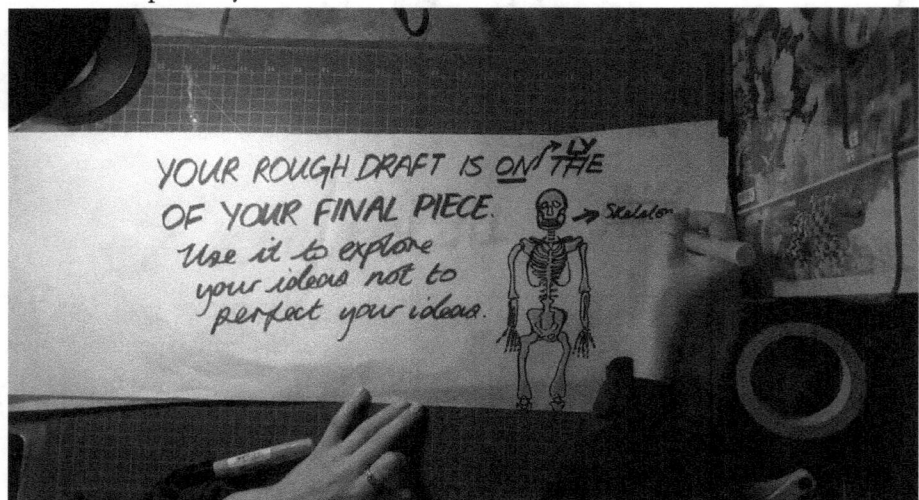

Tip Number 7: Much like an art portfolio where your most successful pieces are at the beginning and end of your portfolio, an essay uses this same technique. Try and make your introduction as powerful and gripping as possible to lure your readers in. Similarly, with the ending- picture it like a dessert- leave them on a sweet note and wanting more.

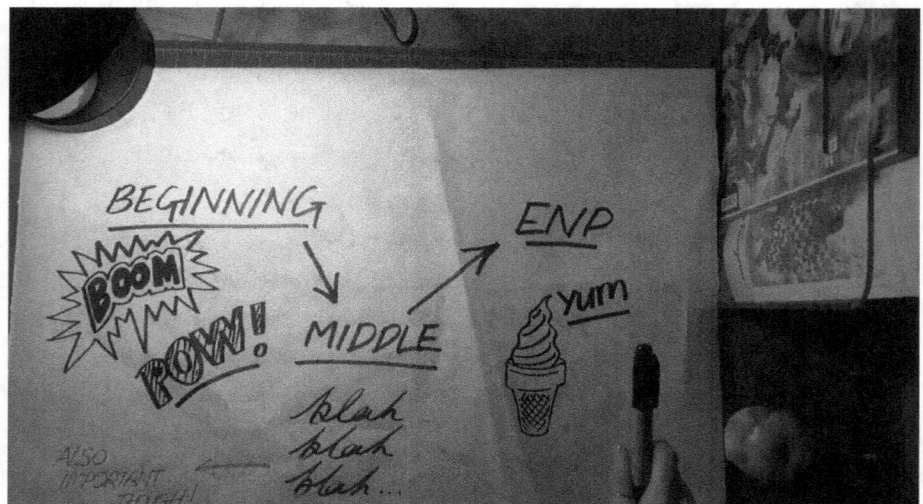

Tip Number 8: Don't be threatened if half your English class are writing/English majors. It DOES NOT necessarily make you the weakest or most inexperienced → Even the most inexperienced can turn out to be the better writers.

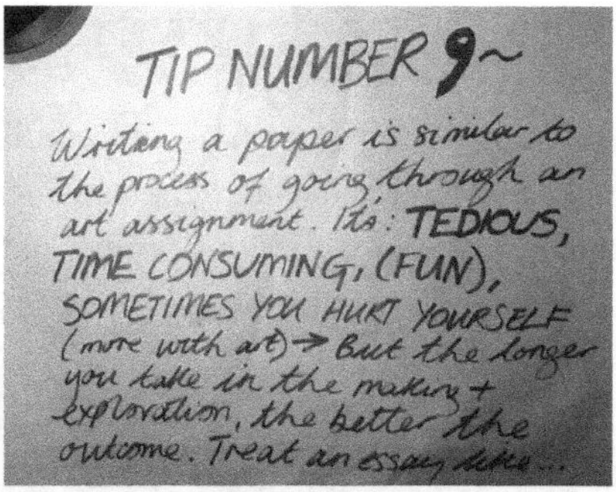

TIP NUMBER 9~

Writing a paper is similar to the process of going through an art assignment. It's: **TEDIOUS**, TIME CONSUMING, (FUN), SOMETIMES YOU HURT YOURSELF (more with art) → But the longer you take in the making + exploration, the better the outcome. Treat an essay like...

Tip Number 9: Writing a paper is similar to the process of going through an art assignment. It's: TEDIOUS, TIME CONSUMING, (FUN), SOMETIMES YOU HURT YOURSELF (more with art) → But the longer you take in the making and exploration, the better the outcome. Treat your essay like... an art project and GET YOUR HANDS DIRTY!

... AN ART PROJECT and GET YOUR HANDS DIRTY!

...

Last but not least: This can apply to everyone: BE YOURSELF.

Every time I've written a successful essay it's because it was personal and from the heart. Use your personal experiences in your writing → it connects you to the reader.

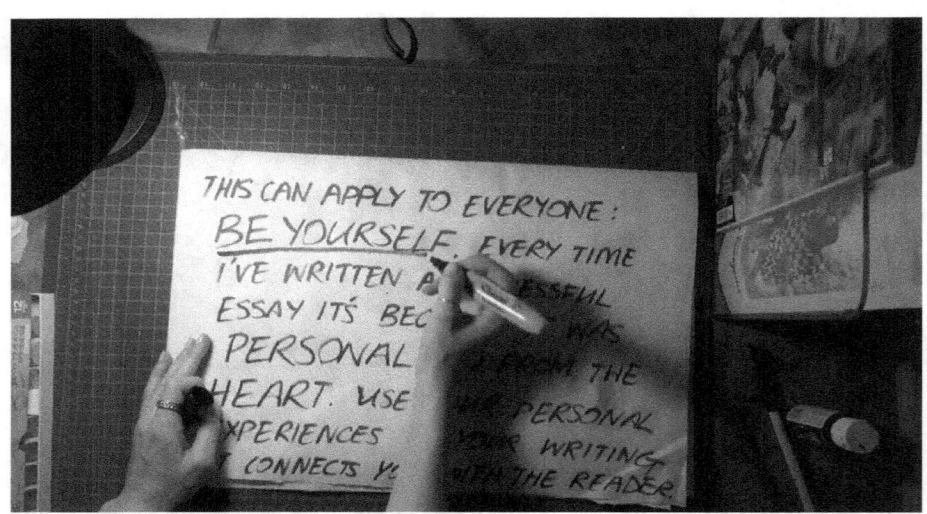

Dyslexia - A Flaw or a Gift

A A B B C C

D D E E F F

G G H H I I

J J K K L L

M M N N O O

P P Q Q R R

S S T T U U

V V W W X X

Y Y Z Z

A page from Daniel Britton, who created the "Dyslexia Font" (Typefaces for dyslexia) in order to help others understand what living with this condition could be like.

Google defines dyslexia as the "general term for disorders that involve difficulty in learning to read or interpret words, letters and other symbols, but that do not affect general intelligence." Initially, this definition surprised me since the part "[does] not affect general intelligence" is often overlooked. You hear the word dyslexia and immediately assume - oh, a learning disability. I believe that this is because exams taken in school don't utilize the strengths of a dyslexic, but actually explicitly tests everything that a dyslexic finds difficult. For my whole life, I've struggled with dyslexia, and felt that the school system has cheated me out of demonstrating areas I am above average in. For example, a major weakness of mine is putting my thoughts into words on paper, not to mention my far below average writing speed, which in any time-based, written exam is crucial. However, after getting some tests done, I've learned that my visuo- spatial reasoning is above 97% of the population. You might now be thinking, your visuo-what? Visuo-spatial reasoning is the "ability to understand visual representations and their spatial relationships." I'm still not entirely sure what this means or how I can prove this strength to be completely honest, but this is exactly the point I'm trying to make. School subjects and tests do not specifically measure or value this aptitude, and therefore, many in a similar position will go unidentified. These students remain under the radar and ultimately 20% who "suffer" from dyslexia drop out of high school and only 67% graduate with a regular diploma.

I believe that the society we live in should stop placing dyslexia in a negative light, which only disheartens those affected, and isn't really helpful to anyone. Instead, we should provide alternative teaching methods, which are more suited to the specific skill set of dyslexics. It may even be possible with the use of different learning techniques to rewire brains and overcome dyslexia. It is also important helpful to remind these dyslexics that their outcomes are not predetermined. Teachers, parents and friends should keep an eye out for those areas they really excel in, (Buchanan, J. 05:01- 05:14).

In case you aren't that familiar with the term dyslexia, I'll explain it briefly. Dyslexia results from a differing in brain structure, which in turn impairs the individual's performance in certain tasks (e.g., having to retain information for long periods of time). This occurs at birth and the cause for it is still unknown. It's also hereditary (Lapkin, E. *Understanding Dyslexia*), which is interesting because now thinking about it, I've often heard my mum complain of her poor spelling - perhaps that's where mine stems from? After reading an article on the Colorado Community Media site called "Dyslexia: Brain Differences and Cognitive Skill Weaknesses," I pulled together some of the common weaknesses that dyslexics share. These include "difficulty with working memory," "poor spelling," "poor comprehension," and an "inability to sound out new or unfamiliar words" (Sevilla, C. *Dyslexia: Brain Differences and Cognitive Skill Weaknesses*). These are just a few of the disadvantages that a dyslexic may have, but each case is specific to the individual and it is really dependent on how severe the case is. It is important to remember that as an individual ages, the brain too changes, and improves, so it is very possible for someone to be born with dyslexia and eventually grow out of it. This can be seen in a study that was performed at Carnegie Mellon University. This study looked into the brains of people who suffer from dyslexia and found through brain imaging that after "100 hours of intensive remedial instruction," their brains were physically "rewired," meaning they had been able to "overcome reading deficits" (McElhinny, K). This is evidence that the brain is flexible enough to adapt. I can back this up with my own evidence as well. I took part in a dyslexia test after my A- level exams (which are secondary school leaving qualifications taken in the UK). Results from my dyslexia test indicated that I was borderline dyslexic at worst, which confused me. I questioned how this could be the case, since my whole life I've been told I had mild-to-mid dyslexia. The examiner told me that it's very common for individuals being tested after intensive exams such as A-levels to come out as non-dyslexic for a short period of time. This is due to the amount of stress, a positive stress, that's been put on the left hemisphere - the "language" hemisphere.

To put it simply, it really is just 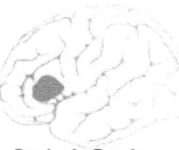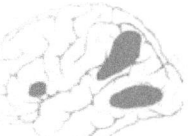 Reading
a massive neurobiological difference
from individual to individual - imagine
it on a scale from mild to severe. Where
I fail other dyslexics may succeed, "no   Dyslexic Reader   Efficient Reader
two cases are the same" (Buchanan, J. 04:49-04:52). Now, here's the science
behind it. The two hemispheres of the brain specialize in particular skill sets. The
left hemisphere is generally associated with language, science, logic, and
mathematics. On the other hand, the right hemisphere is associated with holistic
creativity, music, art, and intuition. Dyslexics rely heavily on the front lobe and
right hemisphere, and generally use the left hemisphere less frequently. The left
hemisphere is activated during reading and is needed in the comprehension and
understanding of words. I like to think of it this way: when we're reading, it simply
takes the connections in our brains longer to travel to the left hemisphere since it's
visited less frequently. For this reason, most dyslexics have "exceptional level of
success in four major vocational path that's entrepreneurship, engineering,
architecture, and the arts" (Bragonier D. 01:58-02:08). Each of these areas rely
heavily on creativity and seeing things spatially in ways that non-dyslexics can't as
easily, essentially meaning that these career paths need individuals with strong
right hemispheres.

It's no wonder that we often see this as a flaw. This is how the story usually
goes. The dyslexic goes through kindergarten and most of primary school with
barely any variations from their classmates or indications of any sort of "weakness."
Then, reading gradually becomes introduced into the curriculum, and in the words
of Dean Bragonier, you essentially "lock the door on 20% of the population" (*The
True Gifts of a Dyslexic Mind*. 03:57- 04:03). This weakness in reading ability
gradually becomes noticed by classmates, teachers and peers. Eventually, dyslexics
have it built into their memory that they are always going to be behind everyone
around them and they just begin to accept this as the case. Teachers may assume
that this weakness comes from a lack of studying or general laziness. It is easy

to see that after each negative test score, homework feedback or peer review the dyslexics' self-esteem will drop lower and lower. In a lot of cases, they persevere with their homework, working far longer than their classmates just to receive the class average. It is truly disheartening. This is why so many call dyslexia a learning disability, a flaw. You can't deny that it's somewhat true, it does make you flawed in certain areas. Without spell-check correcting my spelling, you might laugh at the sheer number of mistakes I've already made at this point in the essay. But I'm not ashamed in the slightest, and I'll accept this is one of my bigger weaknesses. My brain has simply forfeited some areas to create room for major strengths. I'll take that.

There's a link between great achievements and dyslexia. Albert Einstein, Pablo Picasso, and John Lennon all had strong cases of dyslexia. Despite the severity of their conditions, they all managed to go further in their fields than individuals who didn't have this condition. Einstein was said to have such a bad memory that he couldn't even remember all the months in the year.

think different

Meanwhile, he was able to develop some of the world's most complex scientific theories. Steve Jobs is yet another example of using these differences to his advantage. This was illustrated in an advert in 1997 used to promote Apple products. To the right are some of the images that were used to advertise the company. Alongside these images is a minute-long commercial encouraging people to "think different"

(link is to the right). He referred to the individuals in the advertisement as "the ones who see things differently" and "the round pegs in the square holes." It's no wonder that 35% of entrepreneurs, 40% of all self-made millionaires, and 1 out of 2 rocket scientists at Nasa are dyslexic. The society we live in values individuals who can think far outside of the box; with a uniquely "wired" brain (Lapkin, E. *Understanding Dyslexia*), this is more possible with dyslexia. Even with these positive statistics, there's still an unfortunate flip side. Dyslexics account for 50% of all adolescents involved in alcohol and drug rehabilitation and 70% of all juvenile delinquencies (Bragonier, D. 07:17- 08:27). How is it that it seems to go one way or the extreme other? I believe that what determines this is what age we identify the "yes I have difficulties but look what I can do instead." We need to be exposed to situations, at a young age, where our strengths can flourish, to prop up our self-esteem that's being damaged in other ways. We really need help from our peers, our teachers, our families, and our friends to help identify and show us where our strengths may lie (Buchanan, J. 05:01- 05:14).

To further help dyslexics who are unaware of where their strengths may lie, the doctors Brock and Fernette Eide developed an identifier called the "MIND framework," which stands for Material reasoning, Interconnected, Narrative and Dynamic reasoning. I heard of these doctors after watching a TED talk by Jonathan Buchanan called "Stop Climbing, Start Swimming: The Hidden Advantages of Dyslexia." Buchanan explains the framework as follows "Material reasoning: being good at dealing with the physical world. Interconnected: seeing the connections between things. Narrative: putting things into stories, now most people wouldn't think of dyslexics as being particular good authors but strangely they are. Dynamic reasoning: the use of something called episodic simulation to predict how past and future events will occur, something that's incredibly useful for entrepreneurs" (Buchanan J. 05:14- 05:57). This makes complete since entrepreneurs must have exceptional dynamic reasoning to predict potential gaps in the market. This framework is extremely useful to help identify areas that dyslexics might have major success in. Schools can also help these individuals by changing the methods used to teach the curriculum is taught. Tape recorders can be extremely helpful in the classroom environment since many of the issues dyslexics face are reading based. In this way, class instructions could be recorded so students could listen to and replay back, if necessary. Another useful strategy could be to present classwork in small chunks, since often a huge to-do list discourages the students, causing them to switch off. Additional tips include: highlighting essential information, providing glossaries, and blocking extraneous stimuli as some students become somewhat distracted when visuals are placed beside words (Hodge, P. *A Dyslexic Child in the Classroom*)

I performed a small study of my own to see what today's generation thinks of dyslexia. This involved asking 44 people ranging from 17-22 one simple question: Would you consider dyslexia a learning disability? I gave each participant four answers to choose from: Without a doubt yes! Depends on the task at hand. Probably not. No! I send this via text through the website Survey Monkey so all answers remained anonymous. I was genuinely surprised by the results, which I show below in a column chart:

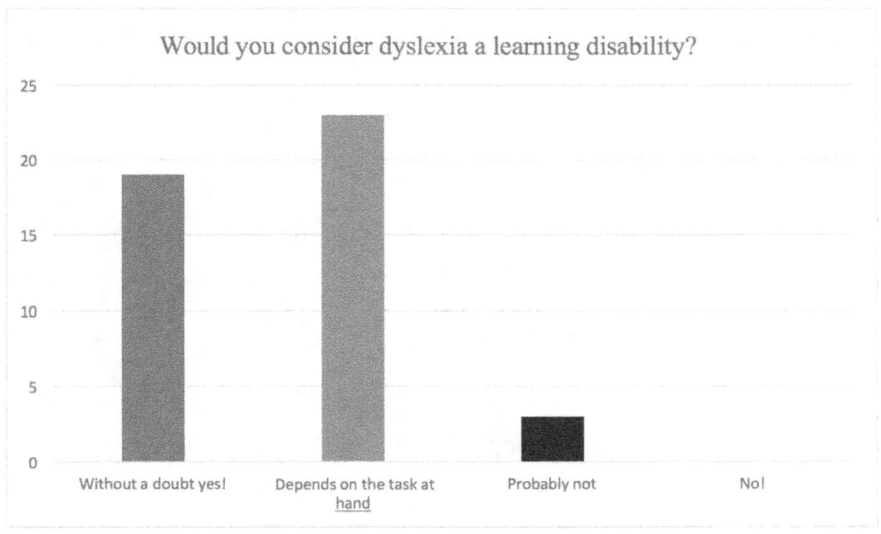

As we can see, the majority believe that it is a learning disability dependent the task at hand. However, most schools, colleges, and universities would disagree and undoubtedly call it a learning disability. Personally, I find the term learning disability somewhat inaccurate, since it is task dependent rather than across-the-board. In addition, it can be disheartening to be categorized as disabled if you are particularly bright some areas. If most agree that it shouldn't necessarily be called a disability, then surely there's a better way to categorize these individuals.

Finally, in the words of Steven McLeish (*The Gift of Dyslexia*. 01:46-01:50), "Why treat a dyslexic differently, if you're not going to teach them differently?" You can't expect them to succeed if you're not going to adapt teaching styles, which is the root cause of their difficulties. I still believe dyslexic students would benefit from receiving additional time as this helps level the playing field. I think it's about time schools embraced these difference and encouraged different learning techniques. Who knows what would happen if the dyslexic drop-out rate fell. We might find a boom in the next generation of amazing entrepreneurs. As Albert Einstein said: "Everyone is a genius. But if you judge a fish on its ability to climb a tree, it will live its whole life believing that it is stupid." (Buchanan, J, 08:00-08:10).

Works Cited

Boer, C. [TEDx Talks]. (2015, November 11). *How a font can help people with dyslexia to read / Christian Boer / TEDxFultonStreet*. [Video File]. Retrieved from https://youtu.be/qVaeGOflF7w

Bragonier, D. [TEDx Talks]. (2015, November 24). *The True Gifts of a Dyslexic Mind / Dean Bragonier / TEDxMarthasVineyard*. [Video File]. Retrieved from https://youtu.be/_dPyzFFcG7A

Buchanan, J. [TEDx Talks]. (2013, March 21). *Stop Climbing, Start Swimming: The hidden advantages of dyslexia: Jonathan Buchanan at TEDxWarwickED*. [Video File]. Retrieved from https://youtu.be/VIIbeqMGB3o

Davis, R. M.Braun, E. (1994). *The Gift of Dyslexia: Why Some of the Smartest People Can't Read and How They Can Learn*. New York, NY: Perigee

Gardner, S. (2013, June 24). *Dyslexia is not a disability- it's a gift*. Retrieved from https://www.theguardian.com

Hodge, P. (2000). *A Dyslexic Child in the Classroom*. Retrived from https://www.dyslexia.com

Lapkin, E. (2016, September 14). *Understanding Dyslexia*. Retrieved from http://www.understood.org

McElhinny, K. (2008, August 5). *Remedial Instruction Rewires Dyslexic Brains*, Carnegie Mellon Study Shows. Retrieved from https://www.cmu.edu

McLeish, S. [TEDx Talks]. (2015, November 1). *The Gift of Dyslexia // Spoken Word // Steven McLeish*. Retrieved from https://youtu.be/5ImEaEK3iKM

Sevilla, C. (2012, July 31). *Dyslexia: Brain Differences and Cognitive Skill Weaknesses*. Retrieved from http://coloradocommunitymedia.com

Stein, J. [Dyslexia International]. (2014, August 9). *The gift of dyslexia*. [Video File]. Retrieved from https://youtu.be/RVseLzwxceM

Typefaces for dyslexia. (2015, August). Retrieved from https://bdatech.org

A Little More Conversation,
A Little Less Texting Please

I see the distant, glazed expression that gradually crosses my friend's face from across the table. Her eyes have moved off mine and now seem glued to the floor. Have I said something? Is something wrong? Her engagement in our conversation has reduced rapidly to "mmms" and "yeahs" dispersed regularly at thirty second intervals. Maybe the conversation has gotten dull, maybe I'm just a boring person. I try to catch her attention with some arm movements. Her eyes flick upwards and she says quickly and rather unconvincingly, "Yeah, I completely agree with everything you're saying" and then once more her eyes are gone, fixated downwards again. Eventually, I ask if everything's okay. After 10 seconds, my words seem to register with her. "Oh sorry, the guy from the party keeps texting me - I don't want to seem rude and ignore him," she confesses. Oh right. Of course. How naïve of me. Of course, she's texting under the table. Great. Once again, I'm talking to a wall.

Nothing infuriates me more than the "texters and talkers." You're hanging out with someone because you've both agreed to spend some quality time with each other. Little did you know that the friend, without asking, has brought along a few others. Even when you think you're having an illuminated phone. Why have they agreed to hang out with just you if they want to have conversations with other people? A way to spot a "texter and talker" is by observing the classic trait they all share - they'll without fail tell you, "You have my full attention." You try to convince yourself that you do have their full attention. They'll even try to convince you again by justifying their behavior, saying "I'm just multitasking." However, I am a strong believer that the term "multitasking" is absolute bullshit. Multitasking just describes getting two jobs done poorly at the same time, in addition to it taking longer. Your full attention is simply split between two tasks; therefore, each gets only half of your attention. This means if you're texting, I'm only getting half of your attention.

What I propose is to favor a more mindful outlook, a society that doesn't communicate solely through texting and that appreciates the sincerity of putting the phone away while in a social situation (e.g., while eating dinner with a friend). Texting while someone else is talking is simply rude and wholly undermines the importance of verbal communication, not to mention you could save a few bucks by saving what you have to say for when you see them!

Now, some of you may wonder why I'm so passionate about this topic considering I am a member of the generation that this disease affects the most. The truth is that I am not opposed in the slightest if someone occasionally checks their phone while you're conversing with them - it's when it gets taken to the extreme. I feel like it's just a small problem that is contributing to an overall bigger issue - the fact that 51% of teenagers would prefer to text someone rather than talk to them in person. That statistic really scares me.

Verbally communicating with someone is SO important, especially as in life practically everything revolves around communication. Interviews, meeting your future spouse, even a house party (no matter how good your moves are) ALL need verbal communication in order to be successful. Why not put your phone down and practice the skill? Verbal communication has meaning and tone behind it, qualities that a text simply doesn't have. For example, sarcasm over text can come across as simply being rude; however, if you were with that person it would be blindingly obvious that they're only joking. This can be very dangerous! Fights can spur from this miscommunication, not to mention the autocorrect fails! It's embarrassment waiting to happen, and why would you want to put yourself through that?

Another reason why I think we shouldn't be relying on technology as much as we are is that it can actually be really expensive. Nearly every teenager these days can be seen with some sort of smart phone, most commonly an iPhone. I was completely gob-smacked when I saw the pricing of the new iPhone 7 when it came out a few weeks ago. It's on average $700-800, and that's just for the handset! Back in the day, when I first got a rather simple flip-phone, I remember when each text message I would send would cost 10p (once 16¢ but now 12¢ post-Brexit). That means ten text messages would cost me £1 which is definitely not insignificant. This meant that I had to cram everything I wanted to say into the 200-character text restriction. It was tragic! I had to abbreviate almost every word and avoid punctuation as this would take up characters. No wonder I've always struggled with correct usage of punctuation. I would even go so far in my texts as to completely avoid questions and anything that would lead the conversation on too much, knowing that this would not only cost the other person money to reply to me, but would force me to respond again, costing another 10p. The horror! However, this was dependent on the pay-as-yougo plan that I originally began with. You can either be on that sort of plan or a monthly arrangement, which involves an outrageous amount being sucked out of your bank account once a month. Sure, it doesn't seem bad month-by-month, but adding up the cost over a year makes it hardly seem worth it. If anything, it makes me want to text more, because at least then I feel like I'm getting my money's worth, which is a ridiculous mindset. On a slightly more serious note, there have been a lot of articles published recently about the worry of how technology is in fact hindering our social development. I guess it's alright to be a "texter and talker" but it should be limited and definitely should not become the only way you communicate. Psychologists worry that many children who haven't yet formed their interpersonal skills are relying too heavily on hiding behind a screen and acting more confident than they really are. After reading a Time magazine article called "We Never Talk Anymore: The Problem with Text Messaging," I found a really strong example of how a text message differs from verbal communication. This example used a text apology and compared it to a verbal apology to pinpoint where certain skills are dropped. In a verbal apology, you are forced to build up courage, look someone in the eye, accept what you've done, and say with meaning in your voice, "I'm sorry." In a text message, you don't need any of these skills, you don't even have to fake an apologetic tone, and you don't have to confront the person. Perhaps, the only intimidating part of an online apology is pressing the send button. The article reveals that "part of the appeal of texting in these situations is that it's less painful – but the pain is the point" and that this pain "leads to better relationships."

This issue has been cropping up everywhere and is getting more publicity. The company Dixie showed that the biggest disruption during a family dinner, is not surprisingly, incoming phone calls and messages. For this reason, they started a project called the "Be More Here" campaign. This consists of pop-up restaurants called "Deadzone Diners," currently only in Los Angeles, which have no cell phone service within the parameters of the restaurant. This forces people to either not bring their phones or to enjoy staring at blank phones with no incoming text messages. The whole meal is completely complimentary just for the price of not using technology. You might be wondering what's in it for the company? Well, they're only offering Dixie food products, so it's helping promote their brand at the same time as making a point. They're even thinking about extending this idea further and making "Zero-Bars," which as the name would suggest, are bars which don't allow any form of technology. Personally, I think that this is a really fascinating idea, but it's sad in a way that you have to make a whole meal free in order to attract the customers. But at the same time, I think it's a really fascinating social experiment and perhaps more of these pop-up restaurants worldwide would help show people the perks of just putting down a cell phone for a simple thirty-minutes and getting rewarded with a free meal!

As my mother once said to me when I used to text while talking to her, I was bringing "ghosts" into the room. That initially made me laugh, but looking back now I actually think it's kind of true. These people I was "talking" to were acting as if they were there in the room with me. These friends I was texting were, in fact, just like "ghosts" - I was the only one who could see them, but their presence could be felt by everyone in the room. She used to tell me she didn't want all these ghosts sitting in our living room when she was talking to me. In fact, it does simply look antisocial, rude, and unengaged and it gives the impression that you'd rather be somewhere else. The true is; you can text your friends anytime, but later, it's too late to go back and spend that quality time! Of course, I'm in the generation of the compulsive texters, but I know there's a time and a place for it - not in the middle of a lecture, not in the middle of a conversation, and not in the middle of a family dinner. Show them you care.

Miles Honey

mileshoney.wordpress.com

Miles Honey
From Writing 100
Nominated by Julie Babcock

The writing in Miles' portfolio is sophisticated, engaging, and does a great job showcasing her interest in art and LGBTQ+ issues. Among the highlights of this portfolio is an analysis of an Alison Bechdel essay, an analysis of the website Autostraddle, and a letter to The Atlantic Monthly that pitches her research project entitled "The College-Educated White Man and the Rise of the White Supremacist."

Julie Babcock

 # Miles Honey

About

Hi and welcome to my digital portfolio! My name is Miles Honey and I'm a freshman at the University of Michigan. I'm currently planning to major in art and design with a prospective dual degree and minor in writing.

from mileshoney.wordpress.com

In addition to my interest in art and writing, I am passionate about animal rights, and I am interested in music, both listening and creating. When I'm not at school, I live in Detroit, Michigan, with my parents and younger sister and our three cats.

my sister in front of our fish pond

my sister's cat Dragon in the garden

So far at U of M I have been focusing on my art classes, but Writing 100 was a great opportunity to rehabilitate my lapsed writing skills while considering pursuing a writing minor. It's really brought back my old passion for journalism (and sometimes even fiction and poetry), and might end up changing my life if I end up following through with my prospective writing minor. I'm excited to see what writing brings me in the future, and in the meantime, I'm excited to share my portfolio with you now!

Project 3: Website Analysis

Autostraddle is a popular blog/website focused on lesbian issues and culture as well as media and entertainment. Unlike much LGBT-focused media and entertainment, Autostraddle makes it a point with every post to include queer women of all identities, with regard to race, sexuality, age, class, and religion. Many trans women, women of color, and disabled women struggle to find representation of queer experiences that look like theirs, be it on similar news-focused sites, or in TV and film. If you're someone who identifies anywhere on the spectrum of queer womanhood who has been disappointed by site after site, Autostraddle is guaranteed to have something to offer you.

Until recently, the site used a more blog feed-like visual format with one post after another, but recently switched to a three column layout that delivers more information to the user from a vantage point. Posts can be accessed in a chronological feed, or from drop-down links split into a few categories at the top of the page (Arts & Pop Culture, Sex & Relationships, Community, Columns, Identities, and More), each of which expands into several meticulously organized subcategories. This row of links is placed under the streamlined logo and site title on the left of the page, drawing the user's eye to it first. To the right are more links to the online store, information about the site, and ways to get involved, as well as donate button highlighted in bright pink, in contrast to the overall white and pale teal color scheme. There is also a search bar and links to all social media at the top of the screen, and a dismissible banner with a more prominent link to the store. The bottom of the screen recapitulates links to the about page, contact information, and social media links, making it easier for the user to access these without having to scroll up again to the top of the page.

Under the "Support Us" link is a drop-down menu with several options. The first, "Buy Our Merch", redirects to another site which hosts the blog's official store where patrons can buy many different designs on shirts, hoodies, and even underwear, ranging from those explicitly declaring one's sexuality to others simply stating a love for cats. The second suggestion offers the option to "Become an A+ Member", the site's premium membership, allowing access to bonus (sometimes personalized) content and deals on merchandise on their own site as well as partnering stores, created to help the site survive without resorting to heavy advertisements. Other options include a simple "Donate" button and a link to shop affiliated businesses from which Autostraddle receives money.

Autostraddle, as mentioned before, is a blog directed toward queer women—specifically lesbians in particular, but the site is accessible and welcoming to women of all sexualities and identities. The creators of Autostraddle make this explicitly clear at every available opportunity, reiterating their mission statement as frequently as possible. The webstore sells dozens of products targeted at women who want to visibly proclaim and celebrate their marginalized identities in loud, colorful ways. The posts on the site for the most part use casual, fun language that is accessible to most ages and levels of education and political literacy, making its content engaging and welcoming for young people with modern sensibilities and unpretentious attitudes toward media. Many if not most posts are directly concerned with LGBT women's issues, some on a serious level (such as issues of homophobic politics, hate crime reports, and poor LGBT representation in media or lack thereof entirely), others on much more entertainment-focused topics (like TV show and movie reviews, comics by lesbian and bisexual women artists, sex toy reviews, and themed playlists). The blog is also heavy on advice columns, usually about sex and relationships but covering everything from pet advice to recommendations for different brands of leggings. The tone is always casual and accessible, and the website design is inviting and cute without being overbearingly cutesy, utilizing stylish but not excessively 'fun' colors and fonts. The site emphasizes intersectional feminism and accessibility as much as possible, always reestablishing its target audience as young adult lesbians, but stressing its inclusivity of all ages and orientations.

Going a step beyond general inclusivity, the site regularly posts writing by and for women of color, transgender women, disabled women and all sorts of women who experience multiple marginalized identities. For example, two comic series on the site, 'Foolish Child' and 'Oh Hey! It's Alyssa' are written by a black queer woman and a physically disabled lesbian respectively and while their comics frequently address their marginalized identities (on top of sexuality), they meander from topic to topic freely, successfully giving platform and voice to women of multiple marginalized identities to discuss both their struggles and just their day-to-day lives, without feeling tokenizing or fetishistic. The site has a clearly accessible drop-down tab of links labeled "Identities", making it easy to find posts pertaining to bisexuality, race, disability, religion, and teenage issues, to name a few of the many identities spotlighted.

Autostraddle takes itself seriously and prides itself on breaking the stereotypical, non inclusive image of the otherwise privileged mainstream LGBT community. Many popular LGBT figures and icons cater to a narrow group of people while pushing down on those more marginalized, but Autostraddle makes it clear that not only are queer women of all identities welcome, they are focused on equally and treated with great importance.

If you're a lesbian, bisexual, or otherwise LGBT+ woman who has struggled with finding a voice and a community on social media and popular websites, Autostraddle most likely has several advice columns, comic series, and miscellaneous blog posts specifically focused on your identity. They also welcome new writers with all different experiences and perspectives, so if you still struggle to relate anything to your specific personal experience, you could be the voice others like you are waiting to hear. Autostraddle exists to amplify the voices of queer women who struggle to be heard.

"Autostraddle Homepage." *Autostraddle*, http://www.autostraddle.com/.

Final Paper and Atlantic Proposal Letter

Dear Atlantic editors,

I am getting in touch to express my interest in writing a feature story for the *Atlantic Monthly*. I read the recent piece 'The Coddling of the American Mind' and while I did not agree with many of its claims, I was impressed by the amount of research and argument simultaneously allowed, and I would love the opportunity to write my own piece for your publication. I've attached the first page of said piece for your convenience.

My piece focuses on the rise of the alt-right movement and its popularity among young, college-educated white men. As a young person who has always spoken against fascism and disguised bigotry, I want to bring to light the insidious ways it invades our society and culture. I've compiled a list of several sources ranging from leftist opinion pieces to posts on white nationalist forums that will help me address this problem from all sides by evaluating every source objectively to see what about it might appeal to its target audience. My plan is to open with some simple facts about the spread of fascist values among educated people, then delve further into the issue with some examples, such as the case of Derek Black, and varying opinions and statements from an array of blogs and journals. I am a first-year student at the University of Michigan and being surrounded by young, educated college students has made me even more interested in this problem. I think my perspective would be a valuable one to add to your repertoire of feature writers.

Thank you for your time,

Miles Honey

The College-Educated White Man and the Rise of the White Supremacist

Before the 2016 election results, the stereotype of a Trump voter was an uneducated, ignorant, politically backwards rednecks and older white Conservatives. However, recent data—in particular, the outcome of the election itself—proves contrary: A large percentage of Trump voters were in fact young, educated men (even women). Further research into this phenomenon shows a trend of these young men coming from much more Liberal-leaning families, often even having grown up with single mothers teaching feminist values (Wilkinson). It doesn't seem to make sense that men with very accepting families and strong college educations would so willfully cast off these equality-focused beliefs in favor of the alt-right, but a close look at the advertising for these movements makes it a little more understandable.

Investigation into the sites that draw in these young men to these movements shows that they often open more innocuously, before leading into propaganda for white nationalism and neo-nazi groups with the claim that to be white in today's society is to be a social beta. For example, many young men find solace for their social awkwardness and lack of skills with women on sites dedicated to "pick-up artistry": constructing the perfect persona and sales pitch to entice women into sex. While morally questionable at best, these forums are much less overtly misogynist than the movements to which they can act as a gateway. These detailed discussions on seducing women and lack of success with women in general often bring up the topic of race, equating sexual prowess with blackness on grounds of racist stereotypes (Wilkinson) and whiteness with "nerdiness" (Osterweil). These claims, while based on insecurity, use race (with a heavy lean on hatred of women) as a scapegoat effectively enough to draw in many seemingly harmless young men and groom them as white nationalists and neo-nazis who firmly support and believe in the calculated racism of the modern alt-right.

SOURCES

Black, Don. "Derek Black Takes the Blue Pill and Renounces White
    Nationalism." *Stormfront RSS*. N.p., 17 July 2013. Web. 22 Nov. 2016.

    https://www.stormfront.org/forum/t981157/

    This is the homepage of the white nationalist site Derek Black was part
    of and his father still runs. The first post at this time is by Black's father
    about his son's detachment from the family's views. While not an article
    about this phenomenon, it could be even more useful to see things
    from these people's own perspectives and get an idea of what about the
    white nationalist/alt-right movement is so seductive to educated people
    (especially men) of all ages. I will definitely find many useful direct quotes
    on this site for my paper.

Bursley, Shane, and Alexander Reid Ross. "How the Alt Right Is Trying to
    Create a 'safe Space' for Racism on College Campuses." *Waging
    Nonviolence*. N.p., 6 Oct. 2016. Web. 22 Nov. 2016.

    http://wagingnonviolence.org/feature/
    alt-right-safe-space-racism-college-campuses/

    This article goes in-depth about young people's (mainly college-age men)
    efforts to bring "alt-right" fascist views to more popularity on college
    campuses. This article is a useful source in that it goes into great detail
    about the history of the more recent fascist movement among young
    people. These young men are the focus of my research and this article
    gives me a lot of relevant information for my paper.

Hunter, Jack. "Meet Milo Yiannopoulos, the Appealing Young Face of the Racist Alt-Right." *The Daily Beast*. Newsweek/Daily Beast, 5 May 2016. Web. 22 Nov. 2016.

http://www.thedailybeast.com/articles/2016/05/05/meet-milo-yiannopoulos-the-appealing-young-face-of-the-racist-alt-right.html

This source features popular young conservative icon Milo Yiannopoulos and explains his appeal to the young alt-right. It is useful for my purposes because it gives an insider's perspective on why the movement can be so appealing to young people. To answer my own questions about why the movement has gained traction among young, educated college students, I need to see things from their perspectives.

Osterweil, Willie. "What Was the Nerd?" *The Left Press*. N.p., 16 Nov. 2016. Web. 22 Nov. 2016.

http://www.leftpress.tk/post/153269939645/what-was-the-nerd

"The myth of the bullied white outcast loner is helping fuel a fascist resurgence," opens this article. This article is virtually the antithesis of my last source—from an openly leftist website, it unambiguously condemns the racism and sexism of this emerging group. While I aim for a broader vision in my own paper, this is useful to see both why this group is gaining traction as well as the effect it has on its social opponents.

Saslow, Eli. "The White Flight of Derek Black." *Washington Post.* The Washington Post, 15 Oct. 2016. Web. 22 Nov. 2016.

https://www.washingtonpost.com/national/the-white-flight-of-derek-black/2016/10/15/ed5f906a-8f3b-11e6-a6a3-d50061aa9fae_story.html

This is a really thorough article on the life of Derek Black, a young man who was raised by and to be a prominent white supremacist leader. He followed his family passionately until moving away to college and experiencing more diversity and making friends who changed his views. While his experience is different from and in some ways even opposite to that of the young men my research is mainly focused on, this will be very useful for analyzing his path away from the conservative white nationalism he grew up entrenched in, and comparing it to the many young men who grow up raised by single mothers and in much more liberal and accepting atmospheres who give in to the pull of white supremacy and misogyny.

Wilkinson, Abi. "We Need to Talk about the Online Radicalisation of Young, White Men." *The Guardian.* Guardian News and Media, 15 Nov. 2016. Web. 22 Nov. 2016.

https://www.theguardian.com/commentisfree/2016/nov/15/alt-right-manosphere-mainstream-politics-breitbart

This article also goes into detail about the alt-right movement's growing appeal to young people and discusses the way it is especially seductive to socially inept young men. This is especially important when looking into why the movement is made up of surprisingly educated people, rather than the ignorant masses. My paper largely focuses on this group and this phenomenon in particular, which is something that most people don't consider since it doesn't fit with their assumptions of what kind of people voted for Trump.

shirt design for the musician Roger Harvey

figure/ink study of my girlfriend playing guitar

a comic from my journal in February 2016

more journal work

portrait of the actress Tammy Blanchard

commissions of a friend's dogs (4 of around 20 dogs drawn!)

www.ingramcontent.com/pod-product-compliance
Lightning Source LLC
Chambersburg PA
CBHW070912030726
47504CB00005B/1568